The Way Of The Virtuous

the Influence
of Art and
Philosophy on
CHINESE GARDEN DESIGN

by Hu Dongchu

 NEW WORLD PRESS

First Edition 1991

Edited by Li Yinghua
Book Design by Yan Xinqiang
Garden Plans by Hu Xiaofen

Published by
NEW WORLD PRESS
24 Baiwanzhuang Road, Beijing 100037, China

Printed by
FOREIGN LANGUAGES PRINTING HOUSE
19 Chegongzhuang Xilu, Beijing 100044, China

Distributed by
CHINA INTERNATIONAL BOOK TRADING CORPORATION
21 Chegongzhuang Xilu, Beijing 100044, China
P.O. Box 399, Beijing, China

ISBN 7—80005—128—5

Printed in the People's Republic of China

FOREWORD

Building gardens is an ancient art. Terraces, pavilions and ponds began to be installed by dukedoms as early as the Spring and Autumn Period more than two thousand years ago. At an even earlier period, the reference in an ancient book to the "failure to secure one final basket of earth in the building of a dirt hill covering over nine *ren* (about seventy *chi*)" obviously pointed to the building of a mound. According to the *Taiping Yulan*, which quoted from the *Sanqin Record*, Emperor Qin Shi Huang excavated three ponds, to which the water of the Weishui River was diverted and which covered an area of four hundred square *li*. The hill of Penglai was also man-made. In the *Record of History*, the *Sanfu Huangtu* relates the construction of a large pond, named Taiye Pond, to the north of the Jianzhang Palace by Emperor Wu Di of the Han Dynasty. The three hills of Penglai, Fangzhang and Yingzhou were then built on three different islets in the pond. History books and other documents amply record the details of such gardens, primarily those attached to imperial residences. Private gardens began to appear after the Wei and Jin dynasties. Though perhaps only half a *mu* in size, the miniature ridges, tree-covered peaks and deep valleys recreated a world of natural beauty. A body of water might further give the impression of a limitless expanse of space.

Painters generally focus on a particular scene to depict their image of nature on scrolls of a limited size. In building gardens, however, nature is actually constructed within a small area. Curving paths, a pine tree, a grove of verdant bamboo, jutting rock and banana trees are arranged as if with the skillful brush of a painter or marvellous pen of a poet describing the Yangtze River. A stroll through one of these gardens reveals an unfolding world of natural scenery, a world so peaceful one is inclined to linger on and lose all sense of time. Many of the imperial gardens and some private gardens, mostly found in Jiangsu and Zhejiang, still exist today.

Professor Hu Dongchu, born in a family of literati, was well grounded in science and reputed to be an erudite scholar. He had a profound knowledge of Chinese history, literature and philosophy and was good at poetry, calligraphy and painting. In his younger years, he visited natural scenic spots and imperial gardens all over China and more recently gathered these materials into a book with descriptive articles and illustrations. I was shown the original manuscript and have enjoyed it very much. The book does not discuss the art of gardening alone but rather probes the thought behind construction, making links to the teachings of Confucianism and Taoism.

In the past several thousand years, there have been Confucianists headed by Confucius, a great thinker, teacher and politician and who has been worshipped by the learned throughout the ages. There have been Taoists of the Taoist school, known as one of the nine schools of thought, who have adhered to the teachings of Huang Di and Lao Zhuang. The long-standing Taoist principles originated from the creed of history-compiling officials concerning honesty, voidness and self-restraint. Professor Hu Dongchu describes in his book the relationship between Confucian and Taoist concepts of the natural world and the art of gardening. The ideas that the learned strive to compare virtues, the wise are fond of rivers, the benevolent are fond of mountains, and benevolence leads to longevity reveal Confucian thought in gardening aesthetics. The Taoist concepts of voidness and quietude have also been reflected in the art of gardening. People of ancient times held that there must be unity between twists and regularities in the layout of gardens. Twists are sought in regularities, while regularities are found in twists. Confucian and Taoist thought are thus pooled together into one entity.

Generally speaking, gardens are places for self-cultivation, sightseeing and rest. But actually, though there were tranquility halls or studies in the imperial gardens, these were not for mental cultivation so much as to ensure the country's administrators enjoyed good health. In the Qing Dynasty the imperial gardens and the Summer Resort at Chengde were political centers, not merely summer retreats. When Fan Zhongyan, of the Song Dynasty, visited the Yueyanglou Tower, he spoke of the need to be the first to share the worries of the country and the last to enjoy its happiness. Sitting in the tower, he did not think to enjoy the landscape but concentrated instead on state affairs and the troubles of the people. In another example, the Zhuozheng-yuan Garden of Suzhou derived its name from a poem by Pan Yue of the Jin Dynasty. He said: "Horticulture is maintained to supply the needs of our meals in the morning and at dusk. This is a way of work in clumsy administration." Degraded in the imperial court, Pan Yue had built a garden to live in seclusion but did not stop thinking about politics. Taoists expounded the management of state affairs through inaction. This inaction, however, must be attained through proper administration. Aside from Confucianism and Taoism, Buddhist art, such as the horizontal boards, couplets, inscriptions, decorative patterns and paintings, has also influenced garden styles in China.

Professor Hu has drawn a wide picture of the natural world. He has painted in the bright points of garden design and written poems lauding the beauty of gardening. His excellent, well chosen photographs pull the reader away from present reality and right into the peaceful realm of the gardens. The album is an excellent piece of work, rich with description and Professor Hu's own photographs.

Professor Hu had asked me to prepare a foreword to his book, but before I had started, he passed away. I have nonetheless written at the request of my late friend, though sorrow has denied me any enjoyment of this work.

单士元

Shan Shiyuan (Professor)

Presiding Member of Academic Committee on History and Theory of Original Architecture of Chinese Architectural Society

President of the Research Society of Traditional Chinese Garden Architecture under the Chinese Cultural Relics Society

Advisor to Palace Museum

September 1989

CONTENTS

Part I

1. Origins of the Art of Chinese Garden Design

Five thousand years ago, Chinese began using hills, streams, springs, plants, and birds and animals to build recreational areas and natural gardens. Later there was an evolution from this simple use of nature to gardens created and managed by man. Three to four thousand years ago, Chinese emperors built great palaces and gardens. For example, in the eleventh century B.C., the King Wen of the Western Zhou Dynasty built the Ling (Divine) Terrace, the Ling Garden and the Ling Lake. The garden covered 17.5 square kilometers of natural forests stocked with all sorts of animals. The king relaxed and hunted in the scenic park. His staff raised fish in the lake, his astronomers used the Ling terrace, a series of tall structures surrounded by a moat, to observe the firmament. From the terrace, the king could admire the surrounding scenery—created by his designers and maintained by his slaves. For all their luxury, these early Zhou Dynasty imperial gardens with their zoos, fish and waterfowl ponds, and observatories were of simple design, and their practical uses far outweighed their entertainment value.

In the Spring and Autumn and Warring States periods of the latter part of the Zhou Dynasty (770-221 B.C.), the Zhou rulers were weak and several dukes and princes took advantage of the situation to expand their power. To aggrandize themselves, they built great gardens in their territories. These gardens centered around tall terraces upon which palatial halls were built. Beneath these "terrace pavilions" streams wound among hills and trees. Some gardens made use of naturally hilly terrain. In this way, plans were drawn up for terrace-pavilion gardens to use the terrain and surrounding environment to enhance the scenery. For example, the King of Wu built the grandiose Gusu Terrace on the banks of Taihu Lake near present-day Suzhou. He used the existing hills in constructing Lingyan Hill Hall, as well as the waters of Taihu Lake and its beautiful islands. This was an early example of the principle of "making use of the scenery of the land." At this time, aside from making use of natural hills and streams, some designers had also begun making hills, a significant step toward man-made gardens. Historical documents of the Zhou Dynasty recorded the adage "failing to build a mound for want of one basket of earth," implying that the prac-

This painting by the famous Ming Dynasty artist Wen Zhengming depicts Wang Xizhi, a great calligrapher of the Jin Dynasty, on an outing in spring when he drank and composed poems together with his friends in the Lanting Pavilion. The hills, rocks, bamboo, water and waterside pavilion in the painting manifest the concept of ancient people on garden aesthetics, that is, to magnify the views in gardens by way of natural hills and water.

tice of hill building had become common enough to enter the language as a maxim.

Central and northwestern China had a thick upper layer of loess covered by rich forests. Early kings and emperors built their capitals in this area because construction materials were readily available, earth being the main resource. Earth was packed to build walls and hills. They used the pits left after the loess was removed to make ponds. Later, this developed into the principle "where there are heights there must be depths," used in the construction of hilly area gardens. However, the man-made hills of this time were all earthen hills; false hills of piled stones had not yet appeared.

An embryonic form of residential gardens emerged as early as three thousand years ago. Buildings in this era were all made of earth and wood, and the overall layout of residential complexes was clearly established. The main building was set on the north edge of a property. The buildings to the east and west were set off against this main building leaving an empty courtyard in the middle. An earthen wall was built up around these buildings with a south gate opening outwards. This basic courtyard layout was retained until recent times. In addition to residences, parks and courtyard gardens were built using a similar design.

The Chinese character for garden, 園 (the original complex form for "garden" pronounced as *yuan*), reflects this design ideographically. The four outside lines signify the earthen walls surrounding the property. The 土 at the top, or "northern edge," of the character signifies the buildings within the enclosure. The small square in the center, 口 , indicates a pond (or empty space) fronted by trees, stones, and hills, which are represented by 衣 . The two characters 園林 (garden and woods) that make up the commonly used word for "garden" can have a very broad meaning. Some of these include: the large garden of pools and hills in a residence; a small residential garden; a villa in the outskirts of the city; a manor in the hills; a secluded residence in the hills; a cemetery garden; a temple garden; a large-scale natural landscape garden; the palace garden of the imperial family; or an imperial resort. All share in common scenery of hills and ponds rich in natural charm and the coordination of many styles of architecture. This contrasts markedly with Western gardens where the center is the focus, and the center typically consisted of a geometrically designed garden and intricately fashioned fountain.

In early times a Chinese residence usually had a garden built to one side or in the back. The garden was divided from the rest of the courtyard by earthen walls and plantings of trees, fruits, and vegetables. There were differences in content, form, and aesthetics, but practical considerations prevailed; few used their gardens for entertainment or leisure. Only later, with the development of culture and art, did the gardens reach their full glory.

2. Confucianism and Daoism as the Soure of Classical Chinese Garden Aesthetics

The outstanding achievement in Chinese garden designing is the unity of natural and man-made beauty. The ideological base for this can be traced back over two thousand five hundred years to the philosophical and aesthetic thought of Confucianism and Daoism.

The Spring and Autumn and Warring States periods saw a great change and cultural boom in ancient Chinese society. A period richer in creativity than any other prior or since, it has been called by Chinese historians the age of "contention of one hundred schools of thought." Confucianism largely influenced the culture, philosophy, and aesthetic thought of the Chinese. Daoism, represented by Lao Zi and Zhuang Zi, opposed and, at the same time, complemented Confucianism. Like two vividly different colored fibers woven together into one strand, this complementary relationship between Daoism and Confucianism is the thread that runs through Chinese aesthetic thought for the past two thousand years.

Confucian and Daoist Concepts of Nature and Garden Aesthetics

Confucian aesthetic concepts put emphasis on the beauty of man-made art and at the same time made use of natural beauty. Daoist aesthetic concepts, taken from nature, held that natural beauty was superior to man-made beauty. Over time, Daoism and Confucianism blended to form China's traditional aesthetic view of natural beauty which became the basis for the design and construction of Chinese gardens.

A major principle used in creating a traditional Chinese garden was that it should harmonize with nature, that the man-made and natural scenes should blend together. Designers placed great importance on preserving and using natural surroundings, not on the large-scale reform of nature by man. Natural characteristics dominate Chinese gardens; man-made scenery coordinates with it, thereby bringing the two together as one. In the construction of large scenic gardens even more consideration was given to how to best utilize nature; extreme importance was attached to the protection of the natur-

The portrait of Confucius engraved on a stone tablet during the Han Dynasty. The stone tablet is now kept at the Wu Family Ancestral Temple of Rongcheng, Shandong.

al environment. The Chinese put emphasis on suiting the scale of the garden to the surrounding terrain and using local conditions to the greatest degree possible. Two thousand years ago, the imperial designers used the principle of "following the flowing water in making the garden" in constructing the imperial palace of the Eastern Han Dynasty (25-220). The main purpose in building a garden was to make use of good terrain, taking environmental factors into account before undertaking suitable alterations. In this way a tradition of gardens with the major emphasis on natural scenery complemented by some manufactured aspects evolved. Thus, the garden came

to embody the merging of Daoist and Confucian aesthetic concepts.

Lao Zi held that the *dao* (way) gave free rein to nature. There being no overriding element, all things developed in their own way as their natures dictated. Forceful human methods were not to be used to damage or change the ecology. For example, the Chinese believed the distinctive shape of the crown of trees was very beautiful. Tree trunks and branches may be straight, slanted, twisted, tall or short, solid or soft; their beauty lay in their variety, a result of natural growth from within and not change forced upon them from without. Western classical gardens stand in stark contrast to this. Westerners clipped trees and bushes into spherical, triangular, square, or animal shapes and called this "green sculpture." They damaged the original natures of the plants, changing their inherent characteristics. The Western mind held that man-made beauty was superior to natural beauty. As a result, manufactured appearances prevailed over the natural, thus marking the fundamental difference between the Chinese and Western systems of aesthetic thought.

Daoist thought upheld nature, proposing a "return to the simple and

the real," a striving to retain the natural form. Alterations by man were permissible, but they must not show any signs of having been crafted. Even what was obviously created by man had to appear natural and real. The garden building principle "though built by man, it appears to come from nature" makes this quite plain. Zhuang Zi's philosophical maxim "though sculpted and carved, return to the simple again" is reflected in the construction of garden hills and ponds that appear to have been naturally formed but are actually the products of meticulous labor.

A common saying among Chinese garden designers went: "A garden that does not yield to hills, streams, and ancient trees but is all the work of man, cannot possibly be of interest. The wonder of gardens is in the use of the scenery, not in the creation of it." Designers took it as a creative challenge to use existing scenery and landscape afforded by the surrounding environment and to develop it to advantage.

From the extant residential gardens in southern China to the imperial gardens in the north, it is apparent that though their situations and conditions differ, none is completely dominated by either nature or man-

A bamboo and stone painting by Zheng Banqiao, a noted painter in late Qing Dynasty. The artist used the hollowness and joints of bamboo to show the modesty and integrity of the literati, while used the hardness of the stone to show their staunchness —all this tends to manifest the realm of thought by way of natural scenes.

made structures. Instead, all share a blending of the two, a merging of man-made scenes with nature.

The Concept of "The Gentleman Copies the Virtuous" and Garden Aesthetics

In Chinese traditional culture, moral education took the place of religion. The aesthetic thought of Confucianism emphasized inquiry into ethical and moral principles. Confucius made aesthetic assessments based on ethical value.

His theory of "mountains and streams equal benevolence and wisdom" is an example. In it, Confucius identifies mountains and streams with ideal moral qualities of people. He once said, "The wise enjoy the streams, the benevolent the mountains; the wise are active, the benevolent passive; and the wise are happy, the benevolent long-lived." To Confucius, the wise see an enterprising spirit and wisdom in the endlessly flowing waters; the benevolent perceive a steadfastness of purpose and unselfish moral character in the lofty and lush aspects of mountains. Associating with nature, one can cultivate a pleasant temperament. Confucius felt natural phenomena could inspire

one to better moral behavior. This emphasis resulted in the development of, and great interest in, mountain and stream poetry, essays, painting, and, of course, hill and pond gardens.

Classical poets and painters often compared a scholar's character and moral integrity with stone, pine, bamboo, plum, chrysanthemum, lotus, and other natural objects. The artist filled the mountains and streams, bamboo and stones with added significance, transforming natural scenery into a reflection of the moral character of the spirit—Confucius' notion that "the gentleman copies the virtuous." The concept came to be a traditional aesthetic point of view used by philosophers and artists to assess a landscape. It exerted such a profound influence on classical Chinese culture and art that the notion became a unique characteristic of the Chinese spirit. To this day, lovers of Chinese classical culture admire and extol nature, often associating it with moral ideals. Because intents and meanings were assigned to natural scenery, the aesthetic, artistic conception of classical gardens was a special embodiment of this principle.

"The gentleman copies the virtuous" became a deep-rooted, second

nature for artists. Classical poets, painters, and garden designers put great emphasis on all forms of quiet and beautiful, grandiose and sublime scenes in a quest to present the viewer with a pleasant image, one that would refine the moral character by persuasion or example. This actualized the Confucian idea of the good and the beautiful united as one. It is the reason why the images of mountains and waters presented never had fierce, evil, frightening, ugly, or desolate aspects that might leave the viewer dispirited.

11

A painting by Wei Xian, an artist in the Five Dynasties (907-960), shows a scholar living in seclusion in a mountain far away from urban life to pursue study. The perfect blend of the scholar's residence and the environment gives a vivid demonstration of the principle of bringing together man's efforts and natural scenes in garden layout.

The piling of cloud-like rocks at the Zhanyuan Garden in Nanjing. Solid stones are brought into harmony with the lovely flowers and plants. In terms of garden construction layout, it depicts the *yin* and *yang* dualism in philosophy.

The Influence of *Yin-Yang* Philosophical Thought on Garden Aesthetics

One of the fundamental traits of Chinese classical garden aesthetics was the opposing yet complementary theory developed from the dualism of *yin* (negative) and *yang* (positive), or *dao*. The Confucian classic, the *Book of Changes* deals with the process of change in all things. It is mainly concerned with the antagonistic yet ultimately united relationships between *yin* and *yang*, hard and soft, and motion and passivity, with the *yang,* or positive, side playing the predominant role. *Yin-yang* philosophy is also a part of Daoism. However, Confucian aesthetic thought focused primarily on ethics and morals, while the philosophy of Lao Zi and Zhuang Zi had its major impact on beauty in art. Therefore, Chinese classical garden aesthetics was largely influenced by Daoism.

Lao Zi believed that all things were in opposing relationships manifested in complementary ways; they stood in contradiction to each other yet were mutually dependent. The effects produced by the contradictory aspects were greater than any that could be achieved singularly. In horticulture, the principles of hard and soft, emptiness and solidity, motion and passivity, crooked and straight, revealed and concealed, simple and adorned, opened and closed, held in and released are all expressions of the dualism of *yin-yang*.

All things have an antagonistic side and at the same time exist in complementary relationship. For example, Chinese classical aesthetic thought held that the plain use of the gentle and lovely was not sufficient, the hard and strong were needed in concert with them. Only then could there be an art object with both bones and flesh. Artists matched hard and strong stones with beautiful, bright-colored peonies in paintings and gardens. The contrast between the two was intended to more fully bring out the beauty in each, the mutually contradictory yet complementary beauty of the whole.

Chinese calligraphy, painting, and poetry put great stress on the effects of strength, of course never so much as to result in crudeness or roughness that did not conform to *yin-yang* aesthetic principles. The ancients said hard and soft blend,

The ancient painting of lotus and rock: In it the simple rock is brought into coordination with beautiful lotus flowers, another example showing *yin* and *yang* dualism, as well as the aesthetical thought of ancient times by way of painting.

mountains and streams are interdependent. *Yang*—hard hills and stones—need to be matched with *yin*—soft waters. Hills and ponds thus became a feature of Chinese gardens.

Separation and connection are fundamental principles behind the layout of southern Chinese gardens. They equate with emptiness in solidity; the spacious empty doors and windows of Suzhou's gardens always open out onto some beautiful scene.

Passivity is contained within motion. That the interchange of the two should produce interest and charm is another feature of Chinese gardens. If hills, cliffs, and rocks simply towered motionlessly, they wouldn't generate any interest. But once they take on some other appearance, either in their natural form or through manipulation, then they acquire a dynam-

ic sense, like a crouching tiger tensed before a leap, thus capturing a vitality viewers can admire. The attitude of ancient trees, the winding of wisteria, bamboo dancing in the wind, slowly flowing streams, birds singing, and fish jumping all lend a sense of energy to the garden. An ancient poet said: "The call of a bird makes the hills more serene." The posture of natural objects and the sounds of birds, waters, and springs intensify the exuberant, life-filled, quiet beauty of Chinese gardens.

Another characteristic of Chinese gardens is the close attention given to simple, unassuming beauty. The simple and magnificent stand together in contradictory yet complementary relationship. The ancient trees, stones, and false hills are matched with the beauty of flowers, plants, and magnificent structures. Often, designers put emphasis on simple and unassuming beauty or gave plain items prominence and supplemented them with a small number of beautiful objects like orchids, wintersweet, ancient trees, and small colored glazed tile pavilions. The emphasis on "simple and unassuming beauty" is a long-held aesthetic concept in China. Confucius admired "beauty of

inherent qualities," "stones refined yet simple," meaning that he saw in the nature of a crude stone a plain and simple beauty. Taihu Lake waters and Huangshan Mountain rocks are important elements in Suzhou's gardens. Their forms and nature are rich in simple beauty. Designers enhanced the inherent qualities of trees and stones; they opposed delicate, affected decorations.

Qionghua Island in Beihai Park of Beijing. On the island is a Lama temple, also known as the White Pagoda. To the south of the island is a winding bridge extending to the shore. The scene is rather magnificent.

Lao Zi emphasized being able to "see intrinsic qualities and simplicity." This is to say that neither the outer nor the inner aspects of a thing possessed ingenious beauty. The outside was like a piece of white silk or an unadulterated knot of wood.

The Influence of the Confucian Concept of "Harmonious Yet Different" on Garden Art

Even before Confucian thinkers had formulated the concepts of "similar objects are not refined" and "all one sound is not pleasant to the ear," meaning that beauty cannot come from singularity, they took the idea of coordination between opposing objects from the *Book of Changes* and expanded it into a philosophical concept of harmony that included all antagonistic or different objects. In line with this theory, the use of one flavor could not result in a tasty dish; sour, sweet, salty, bitter, and spicy flavors must be used in concert. If the amount of each flavor used is just right, a delicious dish will be cooked. The simple use of salt alone will not do; adding some sugar will result in a fresh taste. The appropriate mixing and matching of all types of the antagonistic and different will produce harmony. The harmony of many different things is not unitary, but "harmonious and different." The selection of notes in music, the mixing of colors in painting, the choice of words in writing, and other artistic activities follow the same principles. The bringing together of diversity can produce the most beautiful harmonies. The emphasis on the balanced harmony between different types, the attention paid to synthesis and unity in the arts, and the advocacy of harmonious thought were not restricted to the arts, but also included harmony between man and man, man and nature, and between the elements in nature. In all this can be seen the distinctive nature of Chinese classical aesthetics.

Chinese gardens consist of large and small courtyard-style gardens. Large-scale hill and pond scenery tends to the grandiose; small courtyards work for the delicate beauty small-scale scenery can bring. Some highlight hills, others water, and still others flowers and trees. Some are spacious and open, others quiet and secluded. But each blends together many different elements. Garden structures vary: architectural styles, decorative details both inside and out, all have their own distinguishing qualities. False hills of piled stones can be located by the sides of pools, in the pools, or they can skirt the garden walls. Some hills have structures on them, others are completely scenic false hills with large stones, stone walls, stone statuary, or gullies for streams to run through. They may have caves and passageways in-

side. There may be a pavilion on top of the hill, a stone bridge at its foot, and other characteristics that mimic mountain landscapes in nature. All types of trees, flowers, and plants poke out from between the stones; some flowers and plants float on the surface of the water. The designer brings many different elements together to create a garden, paying careful attention to the matching of different types of hills, pavilions, trees, flowers, and plants. Chinese gardens are the embodiment of the philosophic concept "harmonious yet different."

Because Chinese gardens are composites of many different elements, designers put great importance on developing harmony between differing elements to achieve strong wholistic and synthetic characteristics. The quest for harmony demanded moderation. It was based on the Confucian doctrine of the golden mean which decried extremes and suggested that all manner of elements used in the right degree will achieve balance. Only in this way did designers believe that the various parts of the garden could exist in harmony.

"Emptiness" and "Calm" in Daoist Thought

Lao Zi believed that "emptiness" and "calm" were two aspects of the *dao* of nature. For instance, although a mountain valley was "empty," it was a place where waters could run together; although a room was "empty," its potential stemmed precisely from its emptiness. Lao Zi also said that "something" (like a wall) supplied people with convenience, and "nothing" allowed it to come into use. An empty object was not understood to be void; it was brimming with endless creative possibilities, its potential uses were inexhaustible. Western philosophy, however, em-

phasized the use of solid objects, overlooking the effect of emptiness. Western classical gardens often featured large architectural structures at their centers, a solid core. Southern Chinese gardens often feature an "empty object in the middle": the "empty object" comes from Daoism and the placement at the "center" from the Confucian doctrine of the mean.

Most courtyard gardens are "empty" at their core with scenic objects distributed around the sides. The centers of halls and rooms are also empty; false hills have caves and openings; walls are often punctuated by gates and windows. The designer uses these examples of "emptiness" in the midst of solids (or matter) to enhance the layout of the garden and

the special characteristics of scenery and plants.

Later, Zen Buddhism talked of water as the ultimate mirror, as a condition for the attainment of enlightenment. It was said that empty pools of water had the ability to "hold all objects and situations."

While Lao Zi emphasized "emptiness," he also stressed the effects of "calm" or "quiet." Zhuang Zi said, "Emptiness produces a blank [state]" and a blank state of mind can produce light or enlightenment. He also said, "Water is calm and enlightening; moreover, it has this effect on the spirit." The quiet calm of woods and waters can cause a person's state of mind to come into line with nature, bringing a feeling of contentment and freedom. The mind and the environment blend into one. Daoists believed that tranquility was dominant over impetuosity. Calm and quiet were used as a brake on motion and activity. Leisure balanced labor. A calm, serene garden setting was conducive to a worry-free spirit and, by extension, a longer, healthier life.

Literati of ancient times craved "hills and woods in the city," a quiet, secluded environment in the midst of the hustle and bustle. Confucians believed that a quiet living environment fostered a powerful will, pure and simple personal sentiment, and a balanced life of work and leisure.

Zhuang Zi's Thought on the Relative Nature of Sizes and Horticulture

Daoists believed that all sizes were relative. Something considered of great size is quite small when seen from a broader perspective, they reasoned. On the other hand, what is considered a minute object will be found to be rich in content and form upon closer observation. Moreover, different sizes are suited to their specific uses: the great sun travels the sky in a day, but it cannot enjoy the pleasures of a small bird as it flits over ponds or through bamboo. A small leaf can become a boat that navigates the waters of a small basin.

The comparative nature of size is also an important principle in the construction of Chinese gardens. Designers divide up the space of a garden into large and very small spaces to create scenery that is a pleasant blend of the small and the large. Some call this "a garden within a garden." The large garden encloses a small garden, a large lake also features a small pond, hills and ponds provide large vistas, details enhance the fine touches, the large and the small are a foil to each other. Upon entering the garden, the viewer sees the scenery continually unfolding before him instead of taking in everything at a glance. This is one of the principal aims of the layout of Chinese gardens.

Large gardens have great vistas. Stately, beautiful buildings, terraces, and halls among the boundlessness

In the small Yang Ren Feng Courtyard on the eastern side of the Wanshou (Longevity) Hill one can enjoy the small garden scenes in the Summer Palace.

The Influence of Confucian Emphasis on Etiquette and Order in Residential Gardens

The Confucian system of etiquette put emphasis on balance, symmetry, and rank. The flexible, close-to-nature Daoist concepts combined with this emphasis to guide the overall outer appearance of residential gardens. This is most obvious in the gardens of southern China. They are prime examples of the complementary relationship between Confucianism and Daoism, a symbol of the outlook on life held by the officials and literati of ancient times who looked to Confucianism for outward expression and Daoism for expression of the internal. Southern Chinese residential gardens have a formal, splendid, serious side and a pleasant, quiet, and secluded one, another expression of the contrasting yet complementary systems of thought from which they derive.

Confucian thought focused on cultivating moral character and managing family relationships, having several generations live under one roof, and abiding by a strict system of etiquette. Masters of households were

of nature's mountains and rivers in a large garden bring out the sublimity and majestic beauty of the grand views. Small courtyard gardens have a petite flavor, but the small should not be lost in a quest for the majestic. The hills and plants in courtyard gardens are also greatly intriguing.

A Zen Buddhist poet wrote, "Who knows whether one, two, or three leaves will be better than ten thousand. Knowing only one, two, . or three leaves is enough to know the boundless many." Seeing one red apricot blossom is enough to experience the coming of spring, it is not necessary to wait until the entire tree blooms. One can learn the strength and firmness of a mountain from a single stone; the stone peaks of a ridge can symbolize the might and power of a mountainous terrain. Classical gardens often used the

method of the "small containing the large" in order to bring out the grandeur of nature.

Sometimes designers fitted small courtyard gardens with miniature architectural structures, hills, streams, and pools in order to set up a contrast with mountains and lakes in nature. They also used miniaturization to provide small-scale facsimiles of mountain ranges, the art of creating false hills being an important characteristic of Chinese gardens.

Although Confucianism also laid stress on the combination of *yin* and *yang*, its focus was nevertheless placed on *yang*, as it held that the positive side of things could give to better play of the Chinese people's spirit fearing no hardships and pressing forward under whatever difficult conditions.

The entrance of the Xuyuan Garden through an undulating wall in Nanjing gives one a vivid impression of the Confucianist outlook of life.

dens are free spirited, and scenery is interlinked. But the subtleties can be admired only because attention was paid to the perfection of the whole and the avoidance of confusion.

Gardens of southern China mostly consist of a number of scenic regions which vary in style. "Order," or "alignment," is important for gar-

mostly officials or literati who could not escape the restrictions of family rules of etiquette and live as they pleased. However, they could construct gardens beside or behind their residences, and in these other worlds they could think or repose, write poetry or paint, and otherwise find happiness and relaxation. Some officials and royalty led lives of luxury and pleasure in their gardens. These types of gardens were separated from the formal residence, but linked in the sense that the general layout caused the two to become one, an expression of the traditional Chinese lifestyle that called for living a Confucian outward life and a Daoist private life. Confucianism stressed etiquette and order. Designers planned residences with great attention to "etiquette." "Order" dictated garden layout. For example, southern gar-

Right: The Five-Pavilion Bridge at Narrow West Lake of Yangzhou, originally named Lotus Flower Bridge, was built in 1757. The bridge was built of lime stone. The 12 piers bear the 15-arch bridge structure. Viewed from the approaching bridge, the five square pavilions, with their glazed roofs, look solemn and majestic.

den layout to avoid a disorderly or unsystematic appearance. Designers incorporated a system of "planned art" (or programmed art), called "alignment" in Chinese, into the overall layout of the garden, while the concept of "etiquette" remained the key point in residential design. Upon entering a Chinese garden one is struck by an initial reserve which seems to lure one on to the sights that lie in wait; one proceeds from the shallows to the depths in an orderly manner. One never enters a garden and sees all at first glance; there is always a planned, gradual entry into a realm of rich possibilities.

The arrangement of viewing routes, the layout of scenery, the contrasts between scenic objects, all follow this "order," making it easy for visitors to enjoy the garden from beginning to end.

Below: At the time of full moon each month, one may find a full moon reflected in water at each arch when one views the bridge in front, presenting a marvelous scene. Seen from the side, the bridge looks beautiful and lovely.

Left: Xuyuan Garden in Nanjing is designed with an eye to overall arrangement.

A bird's-eye view of the Beihai, Zhonghai and Nanhai ponds in Beijing presents
scenes of three islands, one in each pond
—Qionghua in Beihai, a pavilion in Zhonghai and Yingtai in Nanhai. They form the
biggest imperial garden in the vicinity of the
imperial palace in Beijing.

3. The Rise of "Mountain and Water" Poetry and Painting and "Mountain and Water" Gardens

About 1,500 years ago, "mountain and water" poetry and painting flourished. These became the theoretical basis and model for Chinese classical gardens.

Beginning with the late Eastern Han Dynasty (25-220) and lasting until the advent of the Tang Dynasty (618-907), China experienced political and social disorder. During the Eastern Jin Dynasty (317-420), the capital was moved to Jiankang (today's Nanjing) on the southern banks of the Yangtze River to avoid invasions and attacks by neighboring border peoples in the North. This southeastern part of China (today's Jiangsu and Zhejiang provinces) was economically richer than the North, the climate was warmer, and there were beautiful mountains and rivers everywhere. Literati, officials, and noblemen fleeing from political persecution and practical difficulties developed a great love of nature here. Some lived in seclusion in the mountains and forests; others moved about visiting the famous mountains of the area. Many were influenced by the philosophies of Lao Zi, Zhuang Zi, and the *Book of Changes* in their appreciation of nature. Their partiality for mountain and river scenery gradually developed into a general mood in society. Their sensitivity to nature helped them discover how closely linked the beauty of mountains and rivers was to their own states of mind, the two blending together in a synthesis of "artistic conception." This discovery corroborated their ideas about Daoist thought regarding natural aesthetics and the benefits of realizing the *dao*. Famous scholars proposed that "hills and streams can lead to *dao*," and a much deeper understanding of the *dao* could be achieved through the observation and appreciation of nature. This increased the general fondness for natural scenery and caused metaphysics and Daoism to be discussed together as one. With this as the cultural background, poetry and painting that described mountains and rivers reached its zenith. Beautiful scenic spots were chosen as sites for residences in the countrysides; gardens that copied the hills and streams of nature were built in residences in the cities; buildings and pavilions were built beside rivers or on mountainsides; the building of temples on famous mountains contributed to a practice that became more widespread as time passed. Mountains, rivers, springs, and rocks became "favorites" of the literati; mountain and

When they suffered setbacks or failed in officialdom, Chinese literati in history often resigned themselves to a life of seclusion in mountains. The picture shows a natural scene in which ancient scholars spent their times in poem recitation and zither playing.

river poetry, painting, calligraphy, and "hill and stream" gardens became the main avenues of artistic expression. And, not surprisingly, it was during this period that the garden building principles of "capturing nature" were established.

Over the centuries Chinese art has emphasized the close relationship between man and nature, its main task being to bring spiritual enjoyment derived from natural beauty. A person's state of mind interacted with the mountains and rivers and could achieve a state of harmony between object and self. Western classical art, however, featured man at the center, the main theme being narration. For the most part paintings took ancient Greek gods and religious figures as their subjects; portraits were also important. Natural objects and scenery served as backdrops for human and anthropomorphic characters. Moreover, natural objects often opposed man. This is diametrically opposed to the love of mountains and rivers and near-worship of nature exhibited in Chinese arts through the centuries.

At the beginning of the fifth century, the Southern Dynasties mountain and river poet Xie Lingyun built a residence on the side of a hill on the banks of the Yongjia River in Zhejiang Province. He wrote of it: "On the side of a hill by a river completes the beauty of the secluded residence"; "Enjoy the divine beauty of nature from the towering structure by mountains and rivers"; "Peaks spread over inside the door and a series of mirrors glance before the windows." From his door he could see a brace of cliffs and from the window a water surface that reflected like a mirror. After a careful site selection and by making use of the scenery at hand, Xie Lingyun could admire the beauties of nature from within his home.

The pastoral poet Tao Yuanming of the Eastern Jin Dynasty lived in a simple house. Five willows grew in front of his door. Ancient pines and chrysanthemums grew within his garden. They reminded him that his state of mind could suffer frosts and snows and still not wither, that his character could become even more defiant like that of the pine and chrysanthemum when winter's cold arrived. His home was in the vicinity of the Xunyang River in Jiangxi Province, where in his garden admiring the chrysanthemums he had only to raise his head to see Lushan Mountain towering in the distance. Tao Yuanming's is another example of the fine use of surrounding scenery in the site selection of a home.

Zhang Lun, a scholar official in the kingdom of Northern Wei (386-534), was fond of the wonderful scenery of hill and pond gardens. He copied typical mountain scenery and through manual labor recreated its grandeurs. The scenery consisted of a stretch of high hills complete with paths and ancient trees and plants. He stated that this "man-made scenery appeared to be natural." Further, it is noted in *Southern History* that the residential gardens of many literati and officials "featured many stones and waters, as if in the hills"; "the beauty of the springs and stones held a sense of the natural"; "nature could be seen among the accumulated stones and water flowing among them."

4. The Aesthetic Theories of Painting and the Art of Garden Design

Chinese painting theory makes frequent use of the term "hills and valleys." China has many mountains: the south with its hills and rivers, especially in Zhejiang and Jiangsu provinces, and the north with its grand mountains. Many began to believe the phrase "mountains and waters" was insufficient to encapsulate the physical variety of the land. The poets and painters of the Eastern Jin Dynasty (317-420) felt the phrase "hills and valleys" was more appropriate. "Hills" referred to all protruding and elevated geographic formations; "valleys" referred to all low-lying watery areas or plains. "Hills and valleys" generalized the many shapes and forms of mountains and rivers and served the creative and practical needs of mountain and river poetry and painting.

It was said of those with the ability to write and paint that they had "hills and valleys within their breasts," meaning that with all types of mountain and river scenery in their heads they had the experience and training to write and paint well. A garden designer required the same sensitivities to create outstanding gardens.

This picture shows a stone wall on the shore of a pond at the Zhanyuan Garden in Nanjing. The garden designer entertained the idea of "keeping hills and big ponds in mind" and created a scene of poetry and painting by the shore of the pond.

Bright Moon Over Spring Stream, a painting by Yuan Yao of the Qing Dynasty, gives full play of his artistic imagination. In the painting, the hills, water and palace are all imaginary.

The Aesthetic Principles of "Describing the Mind Through Form" and "Using the Imagination and Attaining the Miraculous"

The great painter Gu Kaizhi and calligrapher Wang Xizhi of the early Eastern Jin Dynasty were close friends. Both were well-versed in Confucianism and Daoism and esteemed the mountains and rivers of nature. Before these two, mountains and rivers acted only as the background for paintings of human figures. Gu Kaizhi was the first to use mountains and rivers as the subjects of his works. When the famous Tang poet Du Fu saw a large painting of Gu Kaizhi's hanging on the wall of a temple, he wrote: "Gu Kaizhi, in that year, painted the whole of Cangzhou on the wall." Cangzhou was a word used to represent China, thus Du Fu was praising the power and grandeur of the landscape painting.

In summarizing his painting experience, Gu Kaizhi used two now-famous lines: "describing the mind through form" and "using the imagination and attaining the miraculous." These became sublime ideals for all painters to strive for and also had a great impact on garden design. "Describing the mind through form" meant that outer form and detail in painting should express the nature, characteristics, and romantic charm of the subject. A simply naturalistic description of details that overlooked the spirit of the piece was not art. This ideal was the source of *shen si* (divine likeness) which became a guiding principle in both classical Chinese painting and gardening. For example, unadorned and heavy pieces of stone were used to create a summit of stones in a garden, but when it came to topping the peak one or two uniquely shaped stones would be laid on and immediately the whole would take on a new look. What had been an awkward hill of stones would suddenly come to life. Therefore, in creating garden hills, designers strove to bring out their character and nature and avoided focusing too much attention on whether or not they looked like real hills or mountains, an impossible and unnecessary task.

"Using the imagination and attaining the miraculous" meant that the artist, through his observation and experience of hills and valleys in nature and his training in art, must make full use of his powers of imagination and, bringing the "hills and valleys in his breast" into full play, devise a composition that would result in art. A direct copy of nature would not do. His materials are real objects, not a blank piece of paper. He must have the "hills and valleys within his breast" and suit the scale of the garden to local conditions, responding to the scenery with which he is faced. However, the principles he uses in his work are the same as those of the artist.

"A Short Distance Equates to One Thousand *Li* "and "Enjoy the Mountains and Waters While Reclining"

The Southern Dynasties artist Zong Bing combined the thought of Confucianism, Daoism, and Buddhism in his person. In his youth he wandered the famous mountains of China, returning to his hometown when he was quite old and could no longer travel. Thereupon, he painted the mountains and rivers he had seen on large canvases and covered his four walls with them. He did not have to exhaust himself wandering anymore, but could stay at home and lie down as he did his travelling. Later artists often did large sectional

paintings for halls which came together to form giant landscape paintings allowing one to view all the hills and valleys without leaving the mats of the hall. By digging pools and erecting hills before the main hall in the residential courtyard, garden designers achieved a similar effect that could be savored from inside the hall. Construction of gardens of this kind began before 1400, thus proving that there was an early connection between garden design and the art of painting.

China's famous mountains are all very big and cannot be seen in their entirety close up. Though the scope of what is seen increases the greater the distance from it, scenery and specific objects diminish in size at the same time. In order to draw Song-

shan or Huashan mountains, painters drew to scale, using the guidelines "Three inches drawn in height equates to several thousand feet, and an expanse of several feet represents a distance of a hundred kilometers." This is what painters of classical times meant by "a short distance equates to one thousand *li*." Painters selected scenery carefully as though from a bird's-eye view and then transferred it onto canvas. Garden designers used the same methods to build hills and lay out water ways.

Traditional Chinese painters consider it proper to paint a pine tree in the shape of a dragon. Will this pine tree at the Tanzhe Temple in Beijing give people such an impression?

Emphasis on "Approach," "Artistic Conception," and "Image"

Chinese landscape painting is not purely the copying of nature, great emphasis is laid on *yi* (intention). "The self creates intention, creation of scenery is random." At the same time the artist seeks order in nature he must express his inner thoughts. First, he must have a *li yi* (approach), a general way of thinking regarding all the natural objects he intends to paint. This must be the basis of all artistic creation—poetry, painting, calligraphy, or the planning of gardens. It was said by the ancients: "Intention is the master of all: if the intention is high, so will be the result; if the intention is common, so will be the result." If the scenery and intention are in harmony, if nature and inner thoughts are united, then the inner mood can be expressed in the creation of scenery, causing the self and objects to blend. The scenery of mountains and rivers thus created is rich in unique characteristics, containing different aesthetic experiences. The viewer responds to all he sees, entering into the work and not wanting to come back out. This state is called *yi jing* (artistic conception). Chinese garden designers also pay great attention to *yi jing*.

Chinese painters were skilled at "paintings depicting ideas." "Depicting ideas" refers on the one hand to the artist describing his own thoughts, and on the other to the artist depicting the joy of life in the scenery that he sees. Though the painting may resemble nature it is not exactly alike, it is an "improvement" on nature by the artist. Garden designers also adopted this principle.

"Image" is not the same as form, it is the use of form to express internal essence (spirit). Works of "imagery" have unique expressive powers and artistic charm. False hills in gardens are a form of "image," realistic yet at same time unrealistic because of the methods used to make them. The scenic power of a tall mountain can be expressed on a small scale because emphasis is put on expressing the mountain's "manner," or mien. "Image" does not seek to capture the definite form of the object but puts emphasis on expressing its meaning through form. Artists of the Yuan Dynasty (1221-1368) painted pines like "dragons" and stones like "tigers." By this they meant the air or manner of the trees and stones because these did not really resemble dragons and tigers in concrete detail. The Daoist saying "Capture the idea and forget the form" has exactly this meaning. "Idea," or "intention," is a special aesthetic concept of Chinese classical art. Its origins can be found in Daoist philosophy, and by the fourth and fifth centuries A.D. the concept was being developed and used in all forms of art.

5. The Theory of Classical "Mountain and Water" Painting and Horticulture

Chinese classical painting theory (including theory, explication, and postscript) was written mostly by famous artists and was based on their reflections and experiences. Their influence extended beyond Chinese painting as garden designers adapted to their use classical painting theory, in particular, "mountain and water" painting theory.

This chapter will focus on the theory of Guo Xi, the Song Dynasty (960-1279) painter of "mountains and waters," but will also examine other theories of painting, selecting important theoretical points for summary, and explication.

According to Guo Xi, "People can travel, admire, tour, and reside in the mountains, but those who travel and admire the mountains will not attain to as much as those who tour or reside in them. Why? Though there may be several hundred square *li* of mountain and river, only a small portion (thirty to forty percent) may be suitable for touring or residences. You must use the subjects that are suitable for touring and residences in your art. The admiration of the forest and springs is just another way of speaking of a beautiful area to tour and reside." Guo Xi says that artists should depict scenery in mountain and river paintings as though they had placed themselves among the mountains and rivers. Painting in which the artist appears to just travel in or admire the scenery is not enough. Poets and painters of ancient times aspired to this state. Chinese garden designers also put the same emphasis on touring among mountains and rivers, on placing the individual within the scenery to be viewed. Among the hills and ponds are pavilions, halls, and terraces that afford places to reside and rest in the midst of the scenery, as if one were really among the hills and forests.

"The desire to capture nature is not greater than the amount of traveling which is forever set forth within the breast." According to Guo Xi, only if one has good training in art, has toured and seen much, and has hills and valleys in the breast, will he be able to attain the effect of "appearing as a creation of nature." It is also necessary to "capture the essence," because "a thousand *li* of mountains cannot be all wondrous, ten thousand *li* of waters cannot possibly include all beauty." The artist of mountains and waters must capture the essence of the scenery before him. The hill and river scenery in gardens must also possess the es-

sence of natural mountains and waters before there can be any excellent scenic effects for viewers to admire. When constructing a garden in a natural environment, attention must be paid to selecting an area that contains this essence.

"The mountain looks different from close up and far away, changing in appearance with each step. From the front, sides, and the back the mountain differs, the more one gazes on it the more variable it appears. This is the result of viewing the mountain from all angles." Chinese mountain and water paintings must encapsulate mountains and waters from all sides and from below and above, incorporating both the overall aspect of the scene and the minute details down to the grass and trees. The touring walkways in a garden twist and turn, rise and fall to enhance people's enjoyment of the scenery of the garden through everchanging angles of vision, distances, and backdrops. An important piece of garden scenery, like a stone peaked man-made hill, must be seen from different vantage points: from below one is impressed by its towering majesty; from above one can admire its form as it stretches out into the garden and observe how the hill interacts with its environment. It is not one aspect, but all which bring out the full scenic effect of any object in a garden.

"A mountain may appear thus in summer and spring, but not so in the autumn and winter: it can be said that the scene changes with the seasons. A mountain may appear one way in the morning and another in the evening, in cloudy and clear weather different yet again." Guo Xi's words apply equally to gardens. Garden scenery is based upon the seasonal characteristics of flowers, grasses, and trees. Special arrangements and layouts emphasize seasonal changes in the garden. During the winter it often snows. Garden designers interspersed yellow and red wintersweet and pine about the snowy landscape to demonstrate their courageous character and to act as a sign of the eventual arrival of spring. They placed pavilions high on hills and at the sides of pools and streams to give viewers different angles from which to see the changing moon's reflections.

With regard to the relationship between hills, water, trees, and architectural structures, these words from

Guo Xi on painting theory apply: "Streams are the arteries of mountains, grass and trees are the air, and pavilions are facial features. Therefore, a mountain must have water to live, grass and trees to adorn it in glory, and pavilions to give it the appearance of vitality"; "Stones are a mountain's bones, while waters its delight"; "A mountain is passive by nature, however, water makes it active; rocks are hard by nature, trees and flowers make them alive."

Painting theory also included the principle of *yuan* (three distances) applied to mountains or hills: gazing up at the mountain's lofty majesty is called *gao yuan* (distance in height); depicting different levels of the mountain or an exploration into its depths is called *shen yuan* (distance in depth); and a straight-on, wide

Both pictures show man-made hills at Huanxiu Villa in Suzhou. The garden designer applied the principle of "seeing the big within the small" to make sightseers feel they are among natural hills and water.

view of the mountain is called *kuang yuan* (distance in vastness). The three-distance method is a way of expressing the four spatial dimensions in creating scenery. Chinese garden designers used the three-distance method in spatial arrangements, resulting in scenic objects being positioned high and low, in clear sight and hidden, or in open and closed formations. Designers also used the method to form hills and ponds and construct the differing shapes and styles of architectural structures. In limited space, use of the three "distance" method had the enlarging effect of "the large exists within the small."

In ancient times, some painters were skilled in depicting "a corner of landscape" or "a section of scenery."

Taking a beautiful corner or section from a complicated and massive scene and rendering it exquisitely often had the effect of causing viewers to associate it with the magnificent natural landscape from which it was taken. This method is called "the small containing the large" and was often used in gardens.

In painting theory, people, animals, and implements all have definite form; mountains, water, rocks, and trees, though of no set form, all have their common principles. These include the ecological principles of hills, rocks, trees, and plants; the stable principles of mechanics; the principles of the coordinating of sizes and proportions of scenic objects; and the principles of harmonization of form of hills and rocks and the

unanimity of their surface quality and feeling (sense). Water has the principles of source and flow, and mountains that of the foot and its slopes. Others include the principles of coordination between flowers, plants, and the climate and the layout of the garden; and the principles of tone and coordination between architectural structures, hills and river, and trees and plants.

The content of Chinese landscape painting theory is rich and complicated and only a few main points have been introduced in this chapter. Any detailed comparison of the art of Chinese garden design and ancient mountain and water painting will show how close the relationship was and how great an influence painting theory had on garden design.

6. Gardens Designed by Poets and Painters

A close connection with painting theory caused Chinese classical gardens to develop into a virtual reflection of poetry and painting. Poetry and painting nurtured the layout and selection of scenery in garden art. Paintings and drawings of landscapes, rivers, springs, rocks, ancient trees, and beautiful flowers acted as blueprints and guides for garden designers and builders. Several painters and poets designed and built their own gardens, transferring their poetic and artistic inspirations into the creation of gardens. Wang Wei, an outstanding poet-painter of the Tang Dynasty (618-907), designed his own garden, the Wang Chuan Villa (Rim River Villa). Wang Wei's works have been acclaimed as "poems in paintings and paintings in poems." He knew both Daoism and Confucianism and also believed in Zen Buddhism. His ink and wash landscape paintings heralded the founding of the *Nanzong* (Southern school) of painting. His naturalistic and fresh poems of mountains and waters were also highly regarded.

At the site Wang Wei chose, the Wang Chuan bends back on itself, almost forming a circle. The site was surrounded on all sides by lush green hills and mountains. Wang Wei built his residence in the col of a mountain and designed over twenty scenic spots by the river bank, at bends in the river, on mountain and hill tops, beneath cliffs, and on beaches. Some had bamboo groves as backdrops, others pines and rocks, still others flowers and plants. He built small, simple architectural structures at these places, all coordinated with their surroundings over a wide area to create special scenic spots. In the evenings, Wang Wei would play his *guqin* (seven-stringed plucked instrument) under the moonlight in pine groves as clear spring water flowed over white stones. He took friends on boat tours, drinking and composing poetry as they went. On the south mountain he released pheasants and raised deer among the streams and springs. All of this was spread out over an area of natural hills and streams and required very little manual labor in the making. Wang Wei used the terrain and the beauties of nature in the original environment. None of this could be separated from Wang Wei's Zen Buddhist philosophical thought and his training and skill in landscape poetry and painting.

The layout of scenic spots at Rim River Villa was similar to, if not based

Very few paintings by Wang Wei, a great poet and artist in the Tang Dynasty, can be found. This painting is attributed to him because it bears the inscription of *Wang Wei's "Xuexitu"* by a Song emperor.

王維雪溪圖

upon, the *jing* (scenery) in landscape paintings. A long scroll-like landscape painting was viewed as it was rolled out section by section, one scene following another, different scenes all coming together into one great whole—like the scenic spots of Rim River Villa. Whether it is the ten scenes of West Lake, the ten scenes of Mount Emei, the "eight scenes of Xiaoxiang" at Dongting Lake, or the small-scale scenic spots in southern Chinese residential gardens, the essential units of all of these parks and gardens is the "scenes" of which they are composed. This is a traditional method of Chinese garden layout design. The famous poet and ink and wash painter of the Ming Dynasty (1368-1644) Xu Wei built a small garden within his residence. The garden consisted of ten scenes made-up of streams and pools, rocks and hills, wisteria, flowers, and several small buildings that broke up the scenery. Xu Wei was also known as "green vine" and "the Daoist of Heavenly Pool" because of the scenery within his garden. In one of his paintings, Xu Wei can be seen sitting in one of the buildings in his garden reading a book. The painting is monographed with "Some buildings tilting to the east and west and a man speaking

with a mixed north-south accent," expressing his dissatisfaction with the stifling social climate of the times in contrast to his free and easy, self-indulgent state of mind. The painting exaggerated the arbitrary positioning of the buildings in the garden.

Wen Zhengming was another poet-painter of the Ming Dynasty. He was known as one of the four famous painters of Suzhou and was famous for his poetry, painting, and calligraphy. Once he made two extremely realistic drawings of residential gardens. It is said they were of his own garden. One drawing depicts a large man-made hill at the side of the residence, the other a layout of rock peaks, ancient trees, and bamboo groves in the vicinity of the residence. These two drawings reflect the characteristics of Ming Dynasty Suzhou residential gardens.

Zheng Banqiao, a famous Qing Dynasty (1644-1911) poet-painter known as one of the "eight grotesques of Yangzhou," had only a very small courtyard in his residence. He wrote: "A very small grass hut, a square courtyard, a few stalks of bamboo, a pile of stones a few feet in height and not much space is occupied, not much cost was incurred. But sound can be heard in the wind

and the rain, shadows seen under the sun or the moon, it communicates to me when I compose poetry over a drink, as a companion when I am at leisure or lonely. Not only I love these few rocks and bamboo, but also they me." In another short tract Zheng Banqiao exhibits the poet-painter's ability to forget himself in his own reveries and the magical effect of whitewashed walls and the

shadows of bamboo. "My home consists of two grass huts, bamboo growing to the south of them. In the summer when the new bamboo shoots come, the green shade attracts one, who is sitting in a small chair in the midst, so comfortable and cool—a field of scattered bamboo shadows, so much like a painting by nature itself! My painting of bamboo was not taught by a master, most was learned among the paper windows and whitewashed walls, under the shadows of the moon and the rays of the sun!"

"The Spirit of Poetry and the Flavor of Painting": The Objective in Planning and Constructing Gardens

Artists of China's classical period often spoke of painting and poetry together, the qualities they held in common. The great Song Dynasty (960-1279) poet Su Dongpo held the view: "the traits of poetry and painting are at one, works of nature, fresh and pure." He not only pointed out the common objective of the two, but also believed "works of nature, fresh and pure" were objectives which both strived to achieve. Good poetry should have the qualities of a painting, and a good painting should have the qualities of poetry. The blending of poetry and painting into one, the interlinking of their concepts, has a very long history in China. Garden scenery must not only be marked by a great similitude to painting, but also must have the flavor of poetry. Achieving "the spirit of poetry and the flavor of painting" has long been the objective in planning and constructing gardens.

Part II

7. Residential Gardens of Southern China

Introduction

China's dynastic governments employed many literati as bureaucrats and many of them built residential gardens which became representative of Chinese classical gardens. For this reason, classical residential gardens are said to have a "literati" quality. Literati of the classical period were well versed in the Confucian classics; poets and writers had to take national exams to enter officialdom. Their lives were enlivened by the gardens they had built in their residences. It was quite common for older, retired officials to search out a good piece of land upon which to build a garden in an environment secluded from worldly troubles. Most of these gardens possessed the magical scenery described in the preceding chapter, fully reflecting the styles and characteristics of garden art.

Luoyang during the Tang (618-907) and Song (960-1279) dynasties and southern China during the Ming (1368-1644) and Qing (1644-1911) dynasties were home to a great number of famous gardens. Designers in these areas developed the two great systems of classical gardens which came to represent the quintessence of Chinese garden art

over the past 1,500 years. However, the gardens of Luoyang have long since been destroyed, a great loss to succeeding generations. Of the gardens in southern China built during the Ming and Qing dynasties, only a few remain. Most are located in Suzhou, Yangzhou, Nanjing, and Wuxi.

Garden building of the kind seen in Luoyang and southern China probably began to develop and flourish during the Eastern Jin (317-420) and Northern and Southern (386-589) dynasties. According to historical records, several hundred residential gardens were built during the four hundred years from the eighth to the eleventh centuries A.D. A Song Dynasty poem records that "there were famous gardens everywhere one went," giving us some idea of the situation. During the Ming and Qing dynasties, Suzhou alone possessed over three hundred gardens. A 1956 survey showed there were still 190 gardens of different sizes in the city. However, many were in serious disrepair or had been put to other uses. After the destruction wrought during the "cultural revolution," a few of the remaining gardens were restored to their original splendor. In recent years, many famous gardens have been repaired

Left: The Moon Pavilion seen from the Waterside Pavilion in the Wangshiyuan Garden of Suzhou.
Right: The rockery to the east of the Waterside Pavilion.

for tourism. From these the glories of southern Chinese gardens can still be seen. The quality and number of gardens in the area of the lower reaches of the Yangtze River cannot be matched in any other part of China today.

Following the Song Dynasty, Luoyang declined. Invasions and numerous wars destroyed Luoyang's gardens. As the political and economic heart of China moved to the south, culture and the arts followed, adding impetus to the development of garden design and construction in southern China. A vast number of exquisite gardens possessing the characteristics of the south appeared in Suzhou, Hangzhou, Yangzhou, Ningbo, and other cities in the area.

Another factor in the shift to the south was a sustained drop in temperatures in the north during the Song Dynasty. Bamboo, plum, and other plants and flowers that could not survive the cold could no longer be grown. The climate became harsh and water supplies insufficient, creating a great deal of difficulty in garden construction. Furthermore, few literati remained; there was a lack of talent necessary to design the beautiful gardens that had been so numerous.

In contrast, southern China had a tradition of building gardens and man-made hills, craftsmen skilled at the manipulation of stone and the building of hills were in great abundance, and, overall, there were a larger number of skilled "gardeners" in the south than in the north. Suzhou, Wuxi, and Wuxing are all located on the shores of Taihu Lake. Stones con-

veniently taken from the lake were used in garden construction. Additional stones could be easily found in the area. Costs were low and material quality was high, another advantage over the north. For these reasons, the art of stone piling and the development of hill and pond gardens progressed rapidly and extensively.

The construction skills and technology of southern China, including woodwork, carving, brick and tile work, furniture manufacture, and ornamental fitting, were all of higher quality than that found in the north. The finely wrought buildings in southern gardens added a great deal of luster absent from simpler northern ones.

The area south of the Yangtze River delta was home to large numbers of poets and painters, and many

famous schools of painting began there. Some painters designed their own gardens. Garden designers themselves were all skilled at painting and used the ideas of painting in constructing gardens, thereby encouraging development and innovation in garden design and art.

Suzhou and Hangzhou were already famous for producing silk, the area about Taihu Lake was rich in produce, the whole region possessed highly developed agriculture, industry, and commerce. Yangzhou was one of the richest commercial centers in the region. For nearly four hundred years, from the sixteenth to the nineteenth century, in quality, quantity and creativity, the residential gardens of southern China were the finest in the nation.

The Basic Characteristics of Southern China Gardens

Following are general characteristics of the gardens of Suzhou, Nanjing, Wuxi, Shanghai, and Yangzhou:

(a) An Abundance of Water Scenery Gardens

Suzhou is located on the lower reaches of the Yangtze River, but also on the shores of Taihu Lake and in an area interlaced with rivers and canals, thus it was known as the "land of waters." During the Ming and Qing dynasties, the city was crisscrossed by canals and alleys. Most houses were fronted by alleys and backed by canals that linked up with waterways outside the city. It was easy to divert water because of

the high water table. Designers made great use of water in Suzhou gardens, a majority of which centered upon streams and pools. Other parts of southern China were also rich in water resources with many cities located on the banks of rivers. To fully exploit the possibilities of water scenery, designers often combined it with man-made hills, trees, pavilions, and Taihu Lake stones, creating many water scenery gardens rich in the beauties of nature.

(b) Characteristics of Hot and Humid Climate Gardens

Suzhou's summer is long, hot, humid, and frequently wet. Winter is short and mild. Affording respite from heat and rain and good ventilation to ease the effects of humidity became requirements that all garden

Left: The Jianshanlou Tower in the northern part of Zhuozhengyuan Garden.

designers had to meet. Pavilions and other small architectural structures, in order to enhance ventilation, did not have walls built between pillars; large halls had a series of large wooden screens in place of solid north and south walls. In summer they could be opened wide with the added benefit of bringing the scenery into the halls. Studies, libraries, and most other garden architectural structures had empty courtyards on two, three, or four sides, improving ventilation and allowing the scenery of each courtyard to be enjoyed from within the building. Windows and doors that opened out onto scenery not only improved ventilation, but also united the scenery on both sides, creating contrasts and enhancing each other. Covered walkways were built over important pathways in the gardens to provide protection from sun and rain, their undulating forms leading one on to other scenic splendors. Flat terraces and open rooms were often placed in areas free of direct sunlight, allowing the viewer to enjoy the garden scenery from the cool shade.

(c) Connections Between Residence and Garden

The part of the residence that reflected Confucian family etiquette was always staid and proper with the main hall in a central position flanked by other rooms on the left and right, their layout and form following set regulations. However, in the garden of the residence, architectural layout was flexible, different forms and styles abounded. The architectural structures of these two

Right: The residencial buildings of Liuyuan Garden, Suzhou (seen from the Quxi Tower and "latticed windows").

parts of the residence contrasted and complemented each other, reflecting the twin influence of Confucianism and Daoism. Southern Chinese gardens were not planned just for pleasure, they were also places of daily activity where architectural styles varied. Their style, layout, direction, position, size, and virtually all other aspects were suited to local conditions and freely used to express different states of the garden. Thus, the contrast between unregulated plans and freestyle layouts and the controlled etiquette of the main hall is one of the fundamental characteristics of residential gardens.

(d) Garden Location and Garden-Residence Location

Because the residences of major officials often consisted of two or more interconnected courtyard complexes extending from north to south, there was a lot of space behind them. Here is where most large-scale gardens were built. Middle-sized gardens were often located off to one side. Small gardens were located within walls between residential structures; actually they amounted to courtyards in their own right.

Residences with large gardens were located mostly in the corners of suburbs away from busy and noisy city centers. These places had more land available, undulating mounds appropriate for gardens, and vast fields and mountain streams which could be incorporated into the garden design. Furthermore, land was cheaper, hence costs to build a garden were much less.

39

A small waterside pavilion at Wangshi-yuan Garden, Suzhou. It is called the Yue-dao Fenglai Ting (Arrival of the Moon and Coming of the Wind Pavilion).

(e) Characteristics of the Garden Within a Garden

Often several different sized courtyard gardens were built inside large- and medium-sized gardens, creating different scenic areas that contrasted with and enhanced each other. Within limited space, more garden views were created this way, the changes in scenery as one strolled through the garden resulted in a feeling of great space. Some courtyard gardens were very small and small-scale scenic objects were often used within them to give the effect of "the large appearing in the small." Linkage between the courtyard gardens and the linked changes in scenery within gardens demanded that they be viewed in their proper sequence. Hence, designers were careful to develop methodical yet complicated and greatly variable touring sequences. Pavilions were erected in advantageous positions in the garden where they could serve both as part of the scenery and a good place from which to view it.

(f) Landscape Characteristics of Seasonal Flowers, Plants, and "Ancient" Trees

The trees, flowers, wisteria, and other plants in large Suzhou gardens offer grand views during the four seasons. A garden may have more than one hundred different varieties of plants and flowers. The color, smell, form, and postural beauty of plants are arranged to bring out the natural charm of each. Trees are grouped in bunches of three to five, tall and short intermingled, not straightened into rows or trimmed into other shapes, but with all their natural patterns and shapes preserved, set off against and complementing each other to create clumps of trees rich in the rhythms of natural beauty.

Famous gardens have many "ancient" trees which form the backbone of the garden, straight and powerful. Their simplicity and rich green colors matched with the hills and stones of the gardens of southern China create unforgettable images. Most of the famous southern Chinese gardens were built in the Ming Dynasty and still boast many trees hundreds of years old.

8. Gardens Centered Upon Streams and Ponds

Water is the most graceful element used in making gardens. A great expanse of clear water can give people a feeling of brightness, openness, and leisurely repose. The atmosphere it creates is just what the aesthetic concept of Daoist philosophy described, the realm to which literati of ancient times aspired. In the better, large-scale gardens, designers used the terrain fully along with all forms of water. Gardens were full of the sounds of running streams and gurgling springs, which added to their natural charm. Garden landscapes were dotted with active and still elements, reflecting the "spirit of poetry and the intention of painting."

Water reflecting the sun's rays can brighten up a courtyard garden. It can highlight all manner of scenery, it can mirror clear days and white clouds, morning sunrises, evening sunsets, and all the changes of the seasons. The pond is "empty," but it becomes "filled" with the scenery bordering it, a characteristic of gardens centered around ponds.

Medium- and small-sized ponds were usually square shaped, but with meandering shorelines. Large ponds emphasized length and, in combination with the trees on the shore, made the pond's surface appear to recede endlessly into the distance. The width of large ponds was subject not only to the physical constraints of the land, but also the demands of visually pleasing proportion. Gardens in southern China often centered around ponds because of their ability to make a limited space seem larger.

This chapter will examine and compare ten famous gardens: Wangshi, Tuisi, Yipu, Heyuan, Zhanyuan, Xuyuan, Yiyuan, Jichang, Zhuozheng, and Liuyuan. Of these the Liuyuan Garden has many ponds and streams, a great variety of scenery, interlinking courtyard-style gardens, and a long history. It is an outstanding example of southern Chinese large-scale gardens.

Liuyuan Garden

Historical Perspective

Liuyuan Garden was built during the Jiajing reign of the Ming Dynasty (1522-1567) and is one of the largest existing classical gardens in Suzhou. Xu Taishi, an official, built the garden in the back of his residence and called it the East Garden. On the west side of the residence he also built a West Garden, later converted into a Buddhist temple.

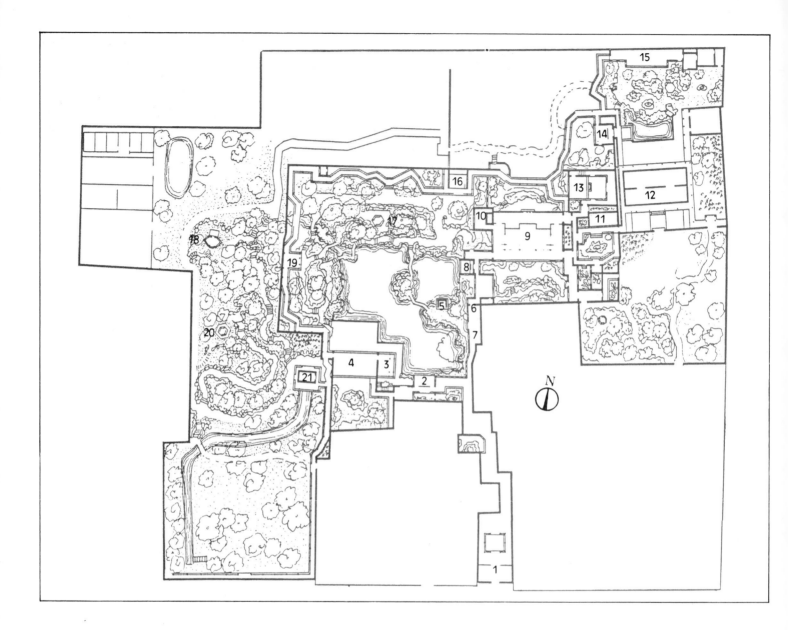

Plan of Liuyuan Garden

1 Main entrance

2 Meadows

3 Mingselou Tower

4 Hanbi Villa

5 Haoputing Pavilion

6 Quxilou Tower

7 Western Tower

8 Qingfengchi Study

9 Wufeng Xianguan (Five Peak Immortal Hall)

10 Jigu Degengchu

11 Yifengxuan (Bow for Peak Hall)

12 Linquan Qishuozi Guan

13 Huanwo Dushuchu Study

14 Xiyu Kuaixue Pavilion

15 Guanyunting Pavilion

16 Yuancui Hall

17 Keting Pavilion

18 Zhileting Pavilion

19 Wenmuxixiang Hall

20 Shuxiaoting Pavilion

21 Huopopodi

The East Garden was also known as the Hanbi Villa (Cold Green Jade Villa). The garden changed ownership often and gradually fell into a state of disrepair until the Jiaqing reign of the Qing Dynasty (1706-1821) when an official named Liu constructed the Hanbi Villa on the foundations of the East Garden. He built the garden with all types of fantastically shaped rocks and stones, which caused it to become quite famous at the time. The central garden of today's Liuyuan Garden and the east courtyard still retain the layout of that period as verified by the Qing Dynasty paintings of the villa. During the Guangxu period of the Qing Dynasty (1875-1909), the scope of the garden was expanded, and it was renamed the Liuyuan Garden. That expansion resulted in the massive layout of today's Liuyuan Garden.

Liuyuan Garden consists of four sections: the central, east, north, and west sections. The central section's hill and water garden is the focal point of the garden; the eastern section's courtyard is set-off against it. Hills and woods are the main attraction of the western section; the northern section was destroyed long ago and has not been restored.

Garden Location and Surroundings

Liuyuan Garden is located outside Suzhou's Beichang Gate in the northwest part of the city where there is plenty of water. The existing garden, including the ancestral temple, covers an area of 25,000 square meters. The garden behind the residence and the courtyard garden have an area of approximately 17,000 square meters.

43

To the east and in front of the garden stands the residence, in the west the ancestral temple, and between the two a narrow corridor, the guest entrance to the garden. This corridor leads to the central section of the garden. The occupants of the residence could enter the garden directly.

During the Ming and Qing dynasties this area bordered on the Shantang River scenic district. Huqiu Hill (Tiger Hill) Pagoda can be seen from within the garden. The hills and streams of the area made it an ideal garden site.

Garden Layout and Scenery Design

The pond is the hub of the central section of the garden and all scenic objects emanate from it like the spokes of a wheel to create a typical closed, circular-style garden. Hills, trees, and architectural structures complement the pond, thus embodying the principle of "uniting man-made beauty and the charm of nature to create wonders" which is characteristic of southern Chinese gardens. The pond's rock shores rise

high above the water, making its surface appear lower. This, combined with scenic objects concentrated around the shores, gives the viewer a lofty, sublime feeling.

Of the scenic objects surrounding the pool, the man-made hill to the north stands out above all others. It faces south and often catches the sun's dazzling rays which give it particular emphasis. From a small pavilion on the peak one can survey the entire garden. To the east and south of the hill, terraces and pavilions dot the pond's shores and contrast with

44

Left: Hanbi Villa viewed from the Quxilou Tower.

the wooded north hill, making it the focal point of the garden.

Chinese garden design tradition placed great importance on the positioning of pavilions and other small architectural structures. A small pavilion in a prominent position not only became the garden's center of attention but also afforded an excellent view of the garden which surrounded it. In Liuyuan, the little pavilion on the north hill is set off against the Yuancui Hall in the rear of the residence and mirrored by the Osmanthus Pavilion on the man-

made hill on the pond's west shore. Though the three are in different locations, they seem naturally related because of their positioning.

Liuyuan Garden's pond is large, oblong-shaped, and stretches between the northwest and southeast corners of the residence. Its wide midsection is in pleasing proportion with the hilltop pavilion on the north shore. Several towers and halls along the southeast shore of the pond lend interest and variety to the landscape. To the east is a small pond with an island connected to the shore by an

angled bridge. The small body of water surrounds the pavilion and creates a separate scenic area. The pavilion is matched with a small stone pagoda, a small stone bridge, small-scale rock pillars on the man-made hill, and scattered clumps of bamboo and flowers to form a miniature water scenery courtyard which contrasts with the much larger hill and pond beyond. Large and small scenic objects and arrangements create visual interest.

The central garden's pond and hills form a complete and separate

garden, an urban scenery of "hills and forests in the city" cut off from the outside world. A covered walkway winds along the northwest garden wall, following the contours of the hill, blocking out sight of the garden wall as it climbs the hill, and reducing any feeling of confinement that seeing the wall might bring.

This garden occupies approximately one-sixth of the residence's area, or about 4,000 square meters. Of this, the pond covers 750 square meters. One may wonder why the pond was not made larger as the water was

plentiful and the terrain placed no limitations on the size of the pond. The answer is simple: the designer made his decision based on the demands of artistic and creative considerations regarding balance and scenic effect.

As a general rule, designers kept ponds to a maximum width of twenty meters, no matter what their shape. This tendency was observed in studies of southern China's large and middle-scale, famous residential gardens. Considering the eye's ability to focus on distant objects, distances

of no more than twenty to thirty meters in any direction seemed to be most appropriate. The size of ponds was related to the garden as a whole. It stands to reason that if the pond was very wide the scenic objects bordering it would also have to be increased in size to maintain harmony and balance—the sense of concentration and the effect of exaggerated perspective would be lost, everything becoming very loose and seemingly orderless. If a large-scale garden had too small a pond, the viewer would feel cramped; an overly large pond

Left: The Guanyunfeng Rock, Guanyunting Pavilion and Guanyunlou Tower viewed from the terrace of the Liangmianting Hall.
Right: An artificial gully built with stones, over which are five stone bridges, as viewed from the southern shore of the Keting Pavilion.

Left: A lower bridge seen from a higher one at the gully.

would cause hills and trees that border on it to lose their sense of loftiness.

Powerful and lofty scenic images were achieved within certain limits, not simply by increasing the size of the garden's pond but by drawing upon the traditions of classical garden design and the principle of "seeing the big within the small." An important part of this was the creation of the three-distance method. Management of space in western classical gardens emphasized flat, uninterrupted distance to create the ef-

fect of limitless size. However, Chinese classical garden designers used the concept of three-distance taken from painting to bring together spatial distance, distance in height, and distance in depth to break the closed-in feeling that might otherwise result.

The central location and substantial width of the pond in the Liuyuan Garden give the sense of open space. Trees on the man-made hill to the north of the pond are all over one hundred years old and reach over twenty meters into the sky, thus

providing the garden with its "distance in height." In the northwest corner where the two man-made gardens come together, water appears to flow out of a deep, wide ravine, thus breaking the penned-in sense that the hills and stones may give and lending a feeling of "distance in depth." Through the use of the three "distances" and the psychology of perspective, the designer has created the impression that the pond and hills have been expanded.

47

Upper: Furniture and interior decorations at the Wufeng Xianguan (Five Peak Immortal Hall).
Right: The transparent partition and furniture at the Liangmianting Hall, or the Mandarin Duck Hall.

Alignment and Path of Viewing

After entering from the street through the main gate, the viewer walks along a winding passageway —at times narrow, at times broad —and enters a radiant, partially-open-to-the-sky courtyard. Latticed windows, through which hill and water scenery can be seen, ornament the north wall of the courtyard and entice the viewer with a prologue to the garden itself.

From here, the main path leads to the west and another small court-yard. Clumps of bamboo, vine, and pelargonium stand in front of the courtyard wall, presenting a pictur-esque scene. Then the path turns to enter a low, dark water pavilion from which the pond and the whole gar-den can be seen in unobstructed day-light. The contrast between the dark interior of the pavilion and the bright garden beyond it leaves a strong im-pression, another example of "seeing the large from within the small."

After leaving the entrance to the garden proper, the viewer skirts a terraced building and arrives at a large hall surrounded on three sides by water. Here the view of the gar-den opens up into a grand vista of hills, trees, buildings, and terraces— the climax of the viewing alignment.

From here one can climb the man-made hill on the west side of the hall. The hill has three levels, the path going up it rises and falls, twists and turns, to offer views of the surround-ing scenery from many different an-gles. From high on the hill, the pond appears much bigger than it really is, another manifestation of "seeing the large within the small."

Upper: The fantastically-shaped rocks and tender bamboo at a small courtyard.
Left: Rocks in grotesque shapes over a flower bed in a small courtyard.

The alignment of scenery in Liuyuan Garden is carefully controlled to disclose more with each step. This intricate beauty—the continual changing of viewing perspective—is also an expression of the poetic intent of "gradually becoming more delightful as one moves along." Chinese garden design has always opposed simple scenic layouts that show everything at once or present clues to the final result at first glance.

Western Section—Natural Scenery Garden

This area covers approximately 5,000 square meters. A man-made hill of earth and stone constructed to look very natural occupies the north side. Its terrain rises and falls and betrays little evidence of having been constructed. The hill sports a grove of maple trees which cover the slopes in green and shade in spring and summer and take on brilliant reds and browns in the fall. Such color is rarely seen in the gardens of

southern China. There are very few architectural structures on the hill. Originally there were three pagodas from which one could enjoy the view of the sea of maples at sunset. These three pavilions have since been destroyed, but two new ones have been built in their stead. To the east of the hill, a whitewashed, undulating wall follows the contours of the hill, rising and falling like the back of a dragon at rest, hence its name, the dragon wall. This wall is also the western boundary of the central section of the garden.

A small stream winds its way past the hill and out of the garden under a stone bridge to the south. Peach and willow trees are planted along both banks of the stream.

East Section—Courtyard Garden

The Five-Peak Immortal Hall courtyard can be entered directly from the central garden. The largest hall in Liuyuan Garden, it is located in the southeast corner of the courtyard and provides an entrance to the garden from the residence, this being where the master lived and entertained guests. The hall is of elegant design. In front of it, against the courtyard wall, there is a hill of piled stone. The hill has five peaks, thus its name. The excellent view of the hill from inside the hall is an example of the principle "without leaving your seat, you can travel through the hills and valleys." The rear courtyard also has a small man-made hill, the walkway that leads past it enters the northern courtyard.

To the east is a small "stone forest" courtyard. If the central garden is a symphony, this courtyard is an instrumental solo. The styles of the two gardens are quite different. By this method of placing small gardens within the larger—"garden within garden"—the designer creates sharp contrasts. To make the transition between the two gradual, a connecting passageway is needed; the Five-Peak Hall serves this purpose.

The "stone forest" courtyard is about 390 square meters. A covered walkway rims the courtyard and defines eight different sized and shaped spaces in which small-scale scenes are created with pillars of stone, banana plants, bamboo, and wisteria. The pillars of stones tower above all else. Gazing up at them from close range produces an exaggerated effect of deformed perspective which makes them appear even more imposing, another example of "seeing the large within the small." The hill and pond garden makes use of the imposing and the grand to create its effects, this courtyard uses the intricate and small to do the same. Both the large garden and the small courtyard use stone to organize their scenery. Though the viewer notices the differences between the two, in the midst of the contrast there exists harmony and coordination.

To the east of the little courtyard, there is a large hall that was built in the final years of the Qing Dynasty. The hall is divided at its center into two sections: the north side provides cool shade in the summer; the southern section contains winter living quarters. Outside the courtyard there had been an opera stage, but it was destroyed long ago. The decorations and ornamentation in this section of the garden are particularly ostentatious and not up to par with the rest of the garden.

Wangshiyuan Garden

The famous Wangshiyuan Garden of Suzhou was built in the twelfth century during the Song Dynasty. The residential garden seen today is a rebuilt version dating from the reign of Emperor Qianlong (1736-1796) of the Qing Dynasty. The garden residence has three sections: the residence to the east; the garden in the center; and the inner courtyard in the northwest corner. Courtyard gardens front and back surround the central pond. The viewer first passes through the tranquil and meandering paths of the front courtyard before entering that part of the garden near the pond where the scenery, reflected in the water, appears bright and cheery. The pond is

Plan of Wangshiyuan Garden

1 Main entrance
2 Sedan chair parking place—Qing Neng Zaoda
3 Jishantang Hall
4 Xiexiulou, a flower room
5 Tiyunshi
6 Wufeng Study (downstairs), and Duhua Tower
(upstairs)
7 Jixuzhai Study
8 Kansongduhuaxuan
9 Dianchunyi
10 Lengquanting Pavilion
11 Yuedao Fenglai Ting (Arrival of the Moon and
Coming of the Wind Pavilion)
12 Zhuoying Shuige Pavilion
13 Xiaoshan Conggui Xuan
14 Daoheguan
15 Zither Room

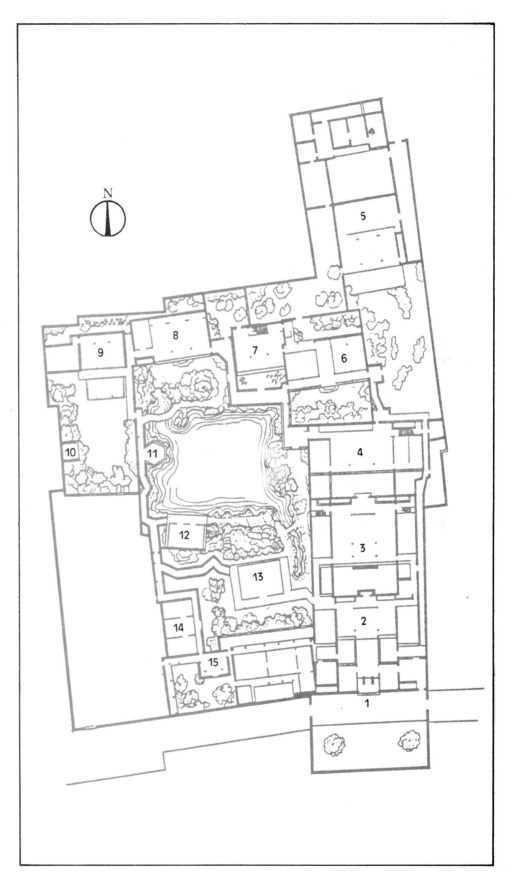

square shaped with some variation in its width, though never more than twenty meters wide at any point.

Here are some of the features the designers incorporated into Wangshiyuan Garden:

1. They arranged scenery at opposite corners of the square pond. Viewed from across the water, the reflected scenery appears more than its actual size. On the southwest side and corner, a tall pavilion contrasts with a low terrace; on the northeast side and corner a water pavilion and connecting walkway stand against a library-study in the background. The result is a magnificent image of the two leaning out across the pond towards each other. Guests entered the garden along the walkway and through the pavilion; the library-study joined the garden to the owner's living quarters. Even today, visitors, upon entering the garden, sense that its layout feels right.

2. The designers placed pavilions near the pond and set halls and the study-library well back from it. This gives the impression of an expansive pond surface, highlights the scenic objects on the pond's banks, and avoids disruption of the scenery. To realize the tradition of contrast between the obvious and the concealed, the designer hid a small courtyard behind trees and rocks on the north shore.

3. In the northwest corner, water flows out of the pond's wide bay through a small stream that passes under a crooked bridge. In the southwest corner, water appears to flow into the other wide bay of the pond from a rocky ravine. The designers used these to relieve the monotony

Left: Yuedao Fenglai Ting viewed from the Kansongduhuaxuan.

Middle: Yuedao Fenglai Ting viewed from the Zhuoying Shuige Pavilion. The Kansongduhuaxuan is behind a small bridge.

Below: The Zhuoying Shuige Pavilion viewed from Zhuwaiyizhixuan across the pond. The front part of the pavilion is over water.

of the square shape of the pond and create a feeling of a deep, expansive body of water.

4. Two ancient pines planted during the Southern Song Dynasty (1127-1279) crowd the rocky northern shore of the pond. Nearly twenty meters high, they harmonize with the buildings to the northwest of the pond and the tall pavilion on its shore to give the garden a lofty aspect. To the east of the pond, the designers set a tall white wall to reflect light and join with the pond in brightening the garden's colors.

53

Upper: The Dianchunyi yard with a painting room.
Left: The scene of Zhuwaiyizhixuan together with the rocks, as viewed from the northern shore of a pond.
Below: Lengquanting Pavilion also known as Banting (Half Pavilion), viewed from Dianchunyi.

5. The designers chose to place the focus of the garden on the pond and use hills as an adjunct. They did, however, erect a stone hill screen on the east shore of the pond and crowned it with wisteria; on the north shore, they built a hill whose imposing grandeur, while subservient to the pond, enhances the delicate beauty of the rest of the garden.

6. The courtyard garden set back from the north bank and the internal courtyard garden in the northwest corner are quiet, secluded areas. The designers created them as retreats in which the owner could read, compose poetry, paint, practice calligraphy, or meet friends. Hills and stones, flowers and trees, and a small pavilion surround the cobblestoned internal courtyard. Its quiet, elegant atmosphere parallels the vibrancy of the water garden scenery, thus

Left: In the rear courtyard of the Kansong-duhuaxuan, shadow of trees on transparent and latticed windows form a beautiful view by itself.
Below: The lattice work on the door of the main hall.

Left: Painting-like bamboo and rock seen from the windows in the northern side of Dianchunyi. The windows are removed in the summer months.
Below: The main hall of the residence with furniture.

achieving the goal of contrast and complement. Originally, this courtyard gained fame from the Chinese herbaceous peony that bloomed there each spring. A long, narrow courtyard behind the study-library in the northern part of the garden contains bamboo and wintersweet among Taihu Lake stones; in summer new bamboo shoots cast shadows by the windows, in winter red wintersweet blossoms dance above the snow. From a seat within the building fresh flowers and green bamboo can be seen throughout the year. Perhaps the quietest and most elegant spot in Wangshiyuan Garden, it is described in an ancient poem: "A room doesn't have to be large to be elegant, flowers do not have to be many to be fragrant."

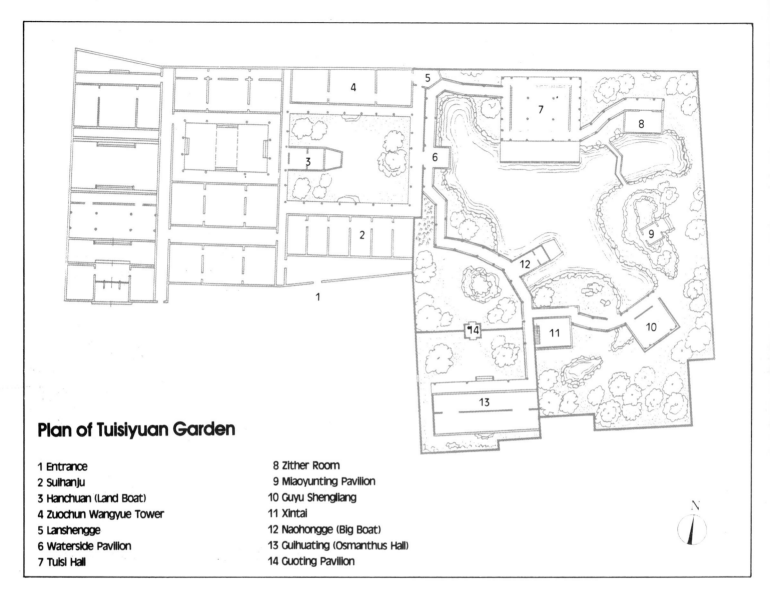

Plan of Tuisiyuan Garden

1 Entrance
2 Suihanju
3 Hanchuan (Land Boat)
4 Zuochun Wangyue Tower
5 Lanshengge
6 Waterside Pavilion
7 Tuisi Hall

8 Zither Room
9 Miaoyunting Pavilion
10 Guyu Shengliang
11 Xintai
12 Naohongge (Big Boat)
13 Guihuating (Osmanthus Hall)
14 Guoting Pavilion

N

Tuisiyuan Garden

Not far from Suzhou in Wujiang County there is a rich and culturally advanced town called Tongli which in the past boasted more than thirty gardens. Tuisiyuan Garden is located there in the southeast corner of an oblong-shaped property. This garden is about the same size as Wangshiyuan Garden and is also centered upon a pond, however there is a great difference in the shape of the pond and the design of the scenery.

Tuisiyuan Garden is unique among gardens of southern China because it has few large man-made hills or tall stone embankments. The water in the garden's pond is almost level with the shore and the structures on the shore all seem to be built on the water. Therefore, some people called it *Tieshuiyuan*, or "close to the water garden." Several characteristics of the design are outlined below:

1. The pond has an irregular shape with several meandering tributaries that branch out through the garden. Water unifies architectural structures,

trees, and stones in the garden, making it seem much more natural than Wangshiyuan Garden.

2. The designer divided the garden into two groups of scenery. Tuisi Hall which is fronted by a flat terrace that comes out to the water's edge dominates the northern part. This is the only large structure of any kind in the garden and it is located at the widest part of the pond. To the east of the hall and cut off from it by a curving, flower-arbor bridge, the Stringed Instruments Room is the most concealed area in the garden. A

Upper left: Rockery in grotesque shape in front of the Waterside Pavilion by the entrance.

Upper middle: Langshengge, where the visitor can have a distant view of the pond.

Upper right: The Waterside Pavilion.

Right: The Untied Boat forms a key scenery together with a small tower and rockery.

small building to the south of the pond connects with a low pavilion by an arched bridge. Before the building, a tall piled rock peak marks the highest point in the garden and counterbalances the buildings to the north. All the pond scenery can be seen from atop the building, and from the hall across the way the beautiful reflection of the peak and the small building can be admired.

3. A red boat-shaped structure, characteristic of Chinese gardens, stands in front of the tower and serves as the focal point for the gar-

den. It appears to lie low in the water. Its juxtaposition next to the tower and pillar of stone unite these elements into a masterful scene.

4. Across from the little red "boat," the designer placed a small stone hill with a pavilion on top for chess playing. This, the Stringed Instruments Room's excellent acoustics, and the little tower's conducive atmosphere for calligraphy and painting testify to the designer's efforts to provide the garden's owner with the means to cultivate his favorite hobbies.

5. The master of the garden served

his guests tea in the Osmanthus Hall to the northwest of the little tower. The area around the hall was planted with sweet-scented osmanthus. A stand of arbor trees behind the tower offered a green backdrop and screened street sounds to make the garden more tranquil.

6. A small courtyard provided a transition to the garden proper. The owner passed his winters in the boat-shaped structure built on dry ground. From here he could admire the lake rocks, wintersweet, and other winter plants scattered about the courtyard.

Yipu Garden

Suzhou's Yipu Garden was built during the middle years of the Ming Dynasty (1368-1644) and still conforms to the original layout. The entrance in the east wall, not the south as was customary, makes this poet's residential garden different from others of its kind. Because the designer placed the garden in front of the residence, the owner could enter the garden directly from the residence's main entrance in the east wall. There

are also several unusual aspects to the scenery in the garden that are worthy of note:

1. A wide pond is the garden's centerpiece. A tree covered man-made hill lies to the south of it, a complex of five halls and pavilions lines the northern shore, and walkways with pavilions along their path run along the east and west shores. In the northwest corner of the pond, a small courtyard is concealed behind a man-made hill.

2. The pond is nearly square and larger than those of Wangshiyuan

and Tuisiyuan gardens. It gives Yipu Garden an air of spaciousness. Bays in both the southeast and southwest corners are crossed by stone bridges. A square pavilion in the southeast corner matches a hexagonal pavilion on top of the hill, an angled bridge and round moon door are located in the southwest corner, and between the two a verdant hill is fronted by the rock lined shore.

3. The man-made hill is made of earth with a cliff of piled stones that forms the face of the hill beneath which runs a stone paved path along

Left: The waterside pavilion in the middle section of a corridor to the west of the pond is a resting place for visitors. There they can also enjoy the scenery around.

Right: A view of the stone bridge and Ruyuting Pavilion.

Below: A courtyard with rockery, a pond and a pavilion.

Lower: Viewed in the yard, both the moon-shaped gate and rockery are reflected in water.

Upper: The rockery built with Taihu stone and a winding stone bridge leading to a neighboring yard through a moon-shaped gate.

the water's edge. After crossing the small stone bridge over the bay in the southeast corner, the path forks: one way leads up the hill passing through a cave before arriving at the hexagonal pavilion on its peak from where the whole garden can be viewed; the other path follows the water to the angled stone bridge, to the west of which is a moon gate that opens into the inner courtyard and the walkway on the western side of the garden.

4. A small, secluded courtyard in the southwest corner of the garden was originally used by the owner as a place to read and write. The library-study burned down long ago, and only a few single-storey buildings remain. There is a small pond of natural cofiguration fed by the large one outside in the main courtyard. Taihu Lake rocks dot its waters. Flowers and bushes planted about the courtyard add a petiteness that contrasts intriguingly with the grand scene of the main garden's pond and hill. The large round moon gate brings the beauty of the scenery on both sides together—a masterpiece of Suzhou frame art. Each view presents a beautiful "painting" of what lies beyond, and brings together the large scene and the small to reflect the Confucian concept of "harmonious, yet different."

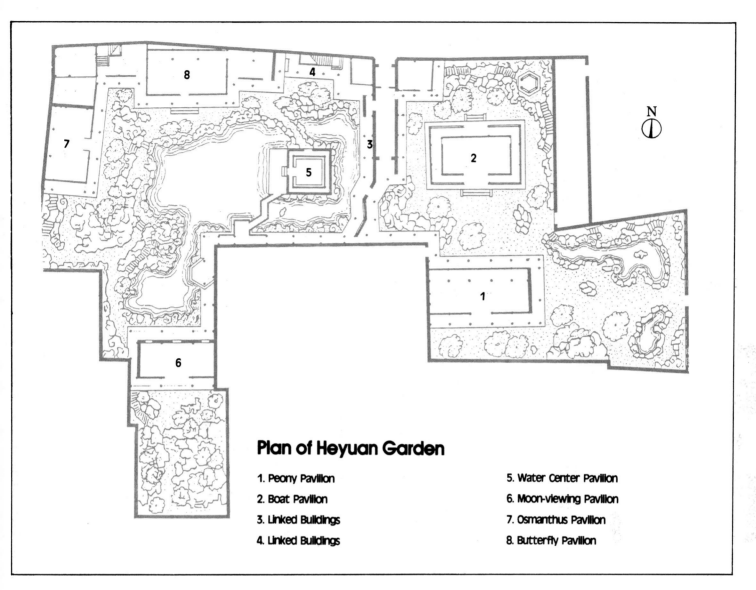

Plan of Heyuan Garden

1. Peony Pavilion
2. Boat Pavilion
3. Linked Buildings
4. Linked Buildings
5. Water Center Pavilion
6. Moon-viewing Pavilion
7. Osmanthus Pavilion
8. Butterfly Pavilion

Heyuan Garden

Yangzhou was a city of rich merchants, and its gardens were quite different in character from those of Suzhou. During the Ming and Qing dynasties there were several dozen famous gardens most of which have since been destroyed by war or fire. Three have been repaired and are now open to the public, Heyuan Garden is one of them. It possesses several unique characteristics:

1. The garden is located behind the residence and is divided into two parts, east and west. The east garden contains a famous man-made hill of piled stones that runs along the garden wall. However, the western part is the focus of the garden. The layout is centered on a pond surrounded on three sides by buildings. A pavilion stands in the water in a central position. To the southwest lies a man-made hill of piled stone. A stream skirts the hill and enters a small scenic courtyard.

2. The pond is oblong, forty meters long and twenty meters wide. A large square pavilion sporting terraces of white stone and linked to the shore on both sides by bridges stands in the middle of the pond and forms the focal point of the garden-pond scenery. Here, the rich merchant owners entertained their guests with feasts and opera, especially during summer when the garden remained cool. The pavilion was used as the stage, thus its name—Opera Pavilion. Music reflected off the pond's broad surface making the sounds brighter. The costumed actors mirrored in the water, especially at night when combined with the light from lanterns

Left: A stone bridge on one side of a square pavilion in the pond.
Below: The residential section in the southern part of the garden.

Below: A winding stone plate bridge on one side of the square pavilion.

and the moon, had a dazzling effect. The second floor of a nearby building gave an unobstructed view of the opera and the garden. Many Yang-zhou gardens followed this pond-centered pavilion layout, a testament to the lives and cultural interests of the rich merchants of the time.

3. The buildings that surround the pond on the north, east, and south sides are known as the "Linked Buildings." Open-air covered corridors connect the buildings across their front rooms. In ancient China, men and women watched opera se-

Upper: Rockery beside a pavilion.

Below: The square pavilion and its two-storyed corridor.

parately—the women on the upper floor, the men below. Outside covered corridors and stairs joined the two levels and kept the audience out of the pouring rain or scorching sun. Walkways on the outside of the linked buildings offered views of the garden from different angles and heights. The linked buildings with their open walls was another unique characteristic of Yangzhou gardens. On the west side of Heyuan Garden there is a square pavilion with walls open to the pines, the columns of rock that tower at the west end of the garden, and the blue sky beyond, thus avoiding any hemmed-in feeling. To the north of the pond and angled to the west is the part of the linked buildings called the "Butterfly." Its central portion bulges like a butterfly's thorax, its flying eaves point high into the air in imitation of the square pavilion below. To the south of the pond, a simple structure of upper and lower covered walkways provides a convenient place from which to view the garden.

4. To the southwest of the pond, a stone paved path winds up a manmade mountain from the water's edge before finally entering a stone cave that takes one to the hill's peak. A picturesque white-bark pine on the hill's slope prompted the ancients to call the hill "the immortal hill upon the sea." The square pavilion in the pond is also called the "square kettle," implying that the garden is the world of gods and immortals. In the water behind the square pavilion a series of oddly shaped rocks juts up out of the water and mirrors the pillars of rocks to the west of the pond.

Plan of Xuyuan Garden

1 Entrance
2 Tongyinguan
3 Yuanyangting (Mandarin Duck Pavilion)
4 Yinxin Shiwu (Stone room)
5 Xiguilou Tower
6 Untied Boat
7 Waterside Pavilion
8 Yilange Pavilion

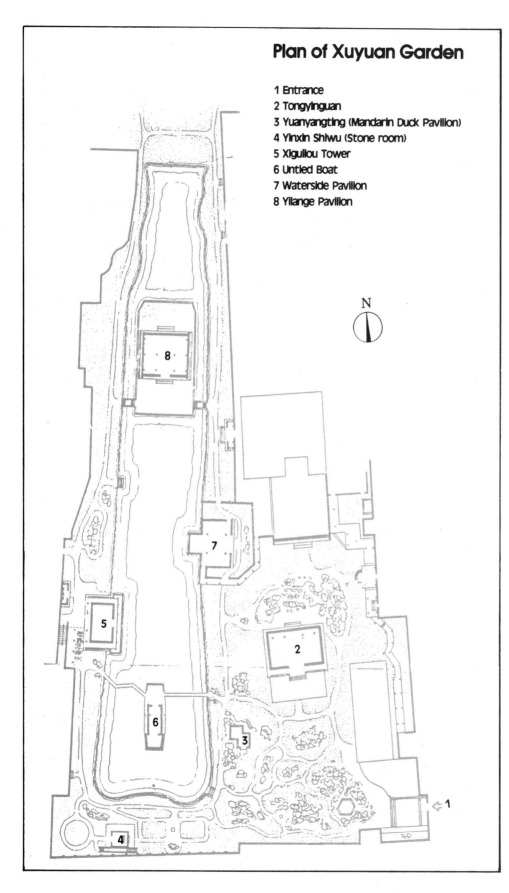

N

Xuyuan Garden and Yiyuan Garden

Before being moved to Beijing at the beginning of the Ming Dynasty, China's capital was located at Nanjing. However, throughout the Ming Dynasty, Nanjing maintained its position as "accompanying" capital, and therefore several royal gardens were built there. Today only two remain, Xuyuan and Yiyuan gardens. Xuyuan Garden has suffered a great deal of damage over the centuries,

and only the central pond section remains. Yiyuan Garden was built during the Ming Dynasty in the sixteenth century and, again, only the water scenery portion of the garden remains. Designers used a stone-boat theme in both gardens, so it is appropriate to compare the two, however, greater emphasis will be placed on the Xuyuan Garden.

Layout and Organization of Scenery

Xuyuan Garden's pond is shaped like a bottle—narrow at one end and widening to twenty meters across. Research has shown that its shape follows that of an ancient stream bed on the site. A stone barge known as the "untied boat" is positioned near the bottom of the "bottle." On the right hand side of the barge, a stone gangplank acts as a bridge to the eastern shore of the pond. A small twisting stone bridge connects the left side of the barge to a small building on the western shore, as if the barge were making a call at a riverside inn and its master was upstairs quenching his thirst. Not far from the mouth of the "bottle" there is a "water" hall with a wide flat terrace which is connected by stone bridges to both banks. Here guests were entertained with music and songs during the evening. The "water" hall and "untied boat" face each other, and their shapes and sizes make interesting contrasts, especially at night when the lighted water hall casts a colorful reflection on the pond.

The "untied boat" rests near the northern shore of the naturally formed pond. It's almost as though the boat is moving slowly down a

river; from the "top deck," one can enjoy the scenery on all sides. The designer erected a waterside pavilion opposite the boat at the south end of the pond, and a plum-blossom-shaped pavilion with a wisteria trellis on the small hill on the western shore. However, the ancient vine and the plum-blossom-shaped pavilion were destroyed a long time ago.

The waterside pavilion in the eastern part of the pond is part of another scene where flowers and shady bamboo crouch along the inner courtyard wall and dip over the

shoreline towards the water surface. The pavilion stands at an angle across from a little red building and complements the "water" hall.

The Origins, Meaning, and Form of the "Untied Boat"

The phrase "floating like an untied boat" in the *Book of Zhuang Zi* expresses the joy of "travelling [in the mind] through emptiness." An aged Song Dynasty poet said of himself "[my] body is like a dried up tree, [my] heart like an untied boat";

though his health was slipping, his mind was still as carefree as a boat cast free upon the waters. The Tang Dynasty poet Bai Juyi often hosted guests on boats in his residential garden in Luoyang. The Northern Song Dynasty poet Ouyang Xiu had a boat built on dry land within his official residence and called it the *Hua Fang Zhai* (Boat of Paintings). He also wrote a poem telling how he spent his life wandering the rivers and lakes of China and recounting the dangerous and happy experiences he had had. He built his "Boat of Paint-

Upper left: Untied Boat at the Yiyuan Garden, Nanxiang County, Shanghai.
Upper right: Untied Boat at the Zhuozhengyuan Garden of Suzhou.

Upper: The stem section of the Untied Boat at the Zhuozhengyuan Garden.
Right: The Untied Boat at the Tuisiyuan Garden of Suzhou.

ings" to remember his past and express his love of life on boats. Later boat-like structures became common features of classical Chinese gardens.

The "untied boat" is not an exact replica of the real thing; rather, it is a composite of many styles of architecture used in gardens made to suggest water craft. Some are like small boats, others like large, two-storey (or more) barges. Most are composed of three parts: the front of the boat is nearly level with the water and used for viewing the surrounding scenery; the mid-section is a room in which guests can dine or rest; and the tail of the boat is raised or consists of a building. Xuyuan Garden's boat is like a flat barge with no building on it, Yiyuan Garden's boat has a small building in the rear. Zhuozhengyuan Garden, which will be discussed in detail later, is famous for its large five-storey boat. In all of these, the designers sacrificed imitation of reality to place emphasis on how the "boat's" form related to its surroundings. This is what garden builders of the past meant when they said:"Form is not restricted, surroundings should be the deciding factor."

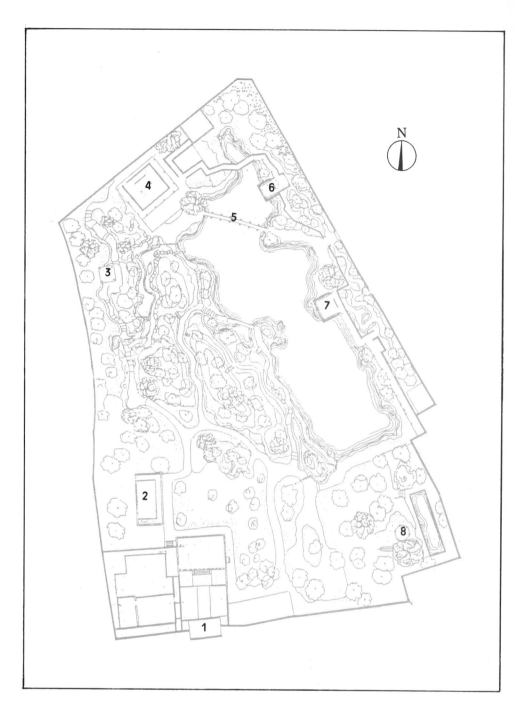

Plan of Jichangyuan Garden

1 Entrance
2 Hanzhenzhai
3 Meiting (Plum Pavilion)
4 Jiashutang Hall
5 Qixingqiao (Seven-Star Bridge)
6 Hanbiting Pavilion
7 Zhiyujian
8 Yubeiting (Pavilion for Stone Tablet Inscribed by
   the Emperor)

Jichangyuan Garden

Located in the eastern foothills of Huishan Mountain in Wuxi, Jichangyuan Garden was known as Huishan Garden during the Ming Dynasty. It was famous for its use of natural scenery and terrain. Upon returning to seclusion in his hometown in 1506, Qin Jin, a scholar-official, chose a piece of hilly, spring-watered land on which to build his suburban garden-villa. Because he included living quarters in the garden, its layout differs from regular residential gardens. Today's garden is rebuilt from the Qing Dynasty version, during which time the streams, gullies, and hills were added. The Emperor Qianlong (1736-1796) visited this garden several times, and he had a replica of it built in the northeast corner of the Beijing summer palace which today is called Xiequyuan Garden. Though Jichangyuan Garden was destroyed towards the end of the Qing Dynasty, it has been restored except for the living quarters which had been located in the southwestern section of the garden. The layout of the garden's

ponds, streams, and man-made mountains are discussed below:

1. The garden is divided into an eastern sector with a long narrow strip of water and a western sector with a man-made hill. A walkway follows the eastern shore of the pond and leads to a waterside pavilion which forms the visual focus of the scenery. Several other small pavilions are scattered about. The walkway and pavilions on the eastern side of the pond afford a clear view of the tree covered man-made hill, as well as Huishan Mountain in the distance.

The man-made hill is built of earth and stone and uses a preexisting slope as a base. Thus, the hill appears to be a foothill of Huishan Mountain. Looking into the pond from its northern end one sees a reflection of the pagoda which stands atop a small round hill on Huishan Mountain.

2. The pond is wide from north to south, narrow from east to west; it averages about twenty meters in width, thirty meters at its widest point compared with only eighteen meters between the waterside pavilion and the large rocks on the op-

posite shore. The pond's shoreline twists and turns, here a bay, there the mouth of a stream. The pond is located on what was once a piece of low lying land. The designer diverted spring waters from the southeast and northwest of the hill to create the pond as it appears today.

3. A long, twisting ravine snakes its way through the northwestern section of the man-made hill. Yellow stone was used on both sides to create walls and mountain cliffs. The designer channelled spring water from Huishan Mountain through

Right: The entrance faces a rockery in the western part of the pond. Mount Huishan can be seen dimly in the distance.

Left: The Jiashutang Hall at the northern end of the pond.

Right: Zhiyujian, a waterside pavilion on the eastern shore of the pond.

Right: The scenery of the garden.
Below: The water pavilion as seen from the northwestern part of the pond. The Long-guang Pagoda on Mount Xishan can be seen in the distance. This serves as a perfect example of "borrowing a scene."

the ravine, filling it with the musical sound of running water and prompting the owner to name it *Bayin Jian* (Eight-Tone Gully). The cliffs are crowned with a thick growth of trees. It is still and quiet within these woods. The secluded, passive aspects of the man-made hill contrast with the open, active nature of the pond and streams. An ancient poem states the relationship well: "When a valley is quiet, springs are even louder to the ear." However, a blockage at the mouth of the spring has slowed the flow of water, and as a convenience to viewers, a winding path has been built in the ravine. As a result, the "Eight-Tone Gully" has lost much of its previous charm.

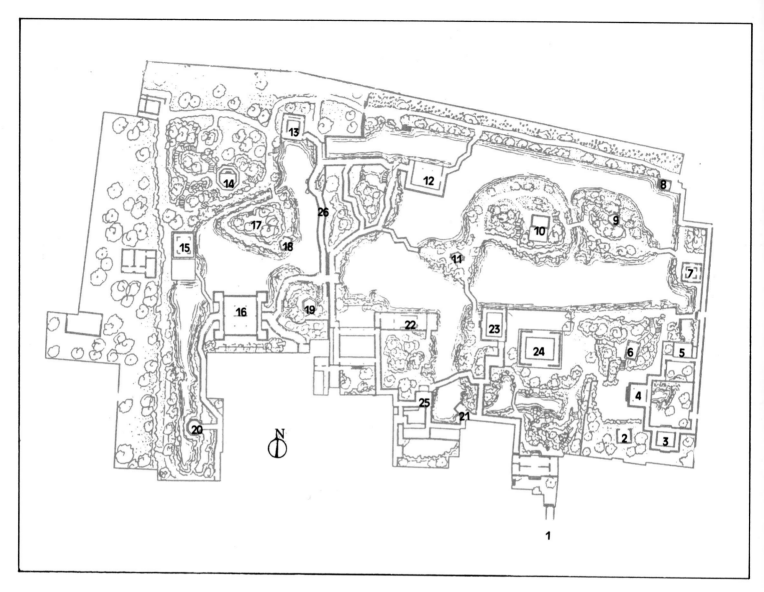

Plan of Zhuozhengyuan Garden

1 Entrance
2 Jiashiting Pavilion
3 Tingyuxuan (Room for Listening to the Rain)
4 Linglongguan
5 Haitang Chunwu
6 Xiuqiting Pavilion
7 Wuzhu Youju
8 Luyiting Pavilion
9 Beishanting Pavilion

10 Xuexiang Yunwei Pavilion
11 Hefeng Simian Pavilion
12 Jianshanlou Tower
13 Daoyinglou Tower
14 Fucuige
15 Liutingge
16 Saliuyuanyangguan
17 Liting Pavilion
18 Shanmianting Pavilion (Fan-shaped Pavilion)

19 Yiliangting Pavilion
20 Tayingting Pavilion
21 Songfengting Pavilion
22 Xiangzhou (Untied Boat)
23 Nanxuan Room
24 Yuanxiang Hall
25 Dezhenting Pavilion
26 A winding corridor over water

Upper: The Xuexiang Yunwei Pavilion viewed from Yuanxiang Hall in the south.
Left: The Yuanxiang Hall seen from the winding bridge.

Zhuozhengyuan Garden

The famous, large-scale Zhuo-zhengyuan Garden is located in the northeastern part of Suzhou and was built in the sixteenth century. Originally the site was a low-lying piece of water-logged land, but after dredging a lake was formed which now takes up seven-tenths of the garden's total area. When the garden was first built in the Ming Dynasty there were few architectural structures, the design emphasized the natural beauty of the ponds and trees. In the early Qing Dynasty, when a high official owned the garden, hills and islands were built, more buildings constructed. The garden today is very much as it was in the early Qing Dynasty. A closer analysis follows:

1. The elongated garden is located behind the residence. A narrow alley passing through the middle of the residence provides entrance to the garden, whereupon a man-made hill obstructs the viewer's vision and a bordering walkway entices the viewer to move on to a quiet, hill-pond scenic area featuring Yuanxiang Hall, the principal structure and center-piece of the garden. Garden architects often used this method of "opening" and "closing" at garden entrances to create desired effects by contrasting wide-open with concealed spaces. Yuanxiang Hall and Nanxuan Room just west of it both stand by the water and form the garden's fulcrum. Across the way from them, there is a pavilion on a small hill-island. The path from the entrance to this spot is the central axis of the garden. The use of a cen-

tral pathway and this type of layout are very rare in southern Chinese gardens. Because Zhuozhengyuan Garden has a rectangular shape, the scenery is logically positioned to maintain control and provide connectedness. The northeast corner of the garden has a courtyard area, the southwest a water-courtyard area, the northwest a pond with covered walkways and buildings surrounding it, and the center a man-made hill with a pond and two small islands upon which are trees and pavilions. Each scenic area works in concert with Yuanxiang Hall in the center of the garden.

2. Yuanxiang Hall has four large windows, one on each side, that afford unobstructed views of the scenery, thus it is also known as the "Four-Sided Hall." In the summer, the lotus on the pond bloom, filling the garden with their gentle fragrance (Yuanxiang means "distant fragrance"). Originally, the man-made hill in the lake facing the hall was planted with wintersweet. Their blossoms covered the hill like snow. The tangerine trees on the man-made hill to the east painted the hill in deep red in autumn. Flowers abounded on the little hill to the south of the pond. Each hill has a pavilion named after the scenery in which it stands. Behind the man-made hill is yet another world—a sea of reeds wave in imitation of the bamboo and trees on the distant northern shore of the pond. Several architectural structures line the southern shore of the pond. Their varying heights and styles add delicate beauty and offer an interesting contrast to the natural scenery of the garden.

Upper: The Wuzhu Youju viewed from Xiuqiting Pavilion.
Upper right: The Wuzhu Youju viewed from Haitang Chunwu.
Right: The undulated corridor over water viewed from the Shanmianting Pavilion.

3. The scenery in the southeast corner consists of three courtyards. The outside courtyard, on both its west and north sides, is made up of a small pavilion on a low mound and a twisting wall which come together to form one compound. The courtyard contains golden-colored thickets of loquats native to Suzhou. A round door at a bend in the wall gives a glimpse of a hill-pavilion and pond, thus extending the spatial dimensions of the small courtyard and bringing the inside and outside scenery together as one. Clusters of *bajiao* (banana plants) located by the banks of a little pond in the central courtyard fill it with lush greenery. The courtyard gets its fame from the sound of rain falling on the banana plant leaves. The rear courtyard is very small, with Chinese flowering crab-apple trees, clumps of bamboo and scenery composed of arranged rocks. A north window in the courtyard's small hall opens onto the water scenery of the eastern part of the garden, thus producing the effect of seeing the large in the midst of the small.

4. A small water-courtyard in the southwest corner uses the rear of the residence which juts out into the garden as a backdrop. The designer channelled water from the southern branch of the main pond into the courtyard. Covered walkways connected to buildings surround the courtyard on three sides. The front of the courtyard is divided from the back by a covered bridge in the middle of which a small pavilion pushes out into the water. From the pavilion one can look past the bridge and out to the small tower in the northeast

Right: The Dezhenting Pavilion as seen from the Songfengting Pavilion in the Canglang Water Yard.

Upper: A small stone pavilion in water beside the undulated corridor over water.
Right: Daoyinglou Tower seen at the undulated corridor over water.

corner of the garden and the "boat" building located in front of the pond. This area contrasts and complements the courtyard scenery in the southeast corner.

5. Today, Zhuozhengyuan Garden consists of the eastern, central, and western sections. Originally, the eastern section had a separate residential garden, but it was destroyed long ago; the western and central sections were originally part of one garden, but they were separated in the late Qing Dynasty when a wall was built to create another residential garden.

Though there are doors in the wall connecting the two sections, their respective scenery is independent of each other and their layouts, originally centered on large waterside pavilions, do not match the narrow confines of the current design.

Close against the dividing wall on the west side is a covered walkway. It not only twists and turns, but also rises and falls like the waves on the pond outside. There is a small tower at the northern end of the walkway, and nearby at a bend in the walkway, a short pavilion stands low to the

water and provides an intriguing contrast to the tower. A fan-shaped pavilion to the west of the pond and extending to the corner of the garden matches the hill-pavilion at the south end of the pond and the buildings and pavilion at the north end. The flowers and trees planted on the pond's west shore and the Wave-Shaped Walkway form a charming water scenery courtyard that is reflected in ever-changing ways upon the waters.

Part III

9. Hill and Rock Landscape Gardens and the Functional Use of Hills and Rocks

Garden designers took natural mountains and rivers as their models, thus guaranteeing a place in Chinese gardening tradition for man-made hills, piled stone pillars, and water scenery. Since the Ming Dynasty (1368-1644), successive generations of garden designers refined the art of building hills and selecting and placing stones. This feature of southern Chinese gardens is now considered one of its most important contributions to classical garden design.

Though an art, the creation of garden hills also has clearly defined methods and guidelines. For example, wondrously shaped large stones are generally placed individually or in small groupings in appropriate spots to show off their beautiful forms. Often used to decorate courtyards, they are known as *zhi shi* (placed stones). Man-made hills are designated according to the materials from which they are built: earth hills, stone hills, or stone and earth hills. Because the ratio of stones to earth of the latter type of hill may vary, stone and earth hills have two subdivisions: earth hills with stones and stone hills with earth. Placed decorative stones have three designations: highlighted stones, scattered stones, and grouped stones.

Hills made entirely of piled stones, within a limited scope, may also have peaks, caves, valleys, rock cliffs, projecting rocks, and other features of hills and mountains in nature. Though these features can be freely mixed and matched, the designer uses them to create hills that establish a feeling, or convey an intention, rather than emulate faithfully the mountains of nature. Most man-made hills are integrated with streams and springs, adorned with trees and plants such as pines, maples, bamboo, and wintersweet, and topped with pavilions as in Chinese landscape paintings. These hills express a composite of the aesthetic thought and artistic interests of classical literati. Unlike earth hills, stone hills are not subject to the limitations of slope angles. Peaks and cliffs may tower aloft, thus creating in a small space an imposing scenic image. Stone hills may hold caves in their depths. Caves can link a hill's outward spatial appearance with its inner nature, they can alter the heavy feeling of a solid hill by changing its character to more closely match that of the rest of the garden. Using the hill's inner environment is called creating latent space.

The rainy climate of southern China makes earth hills an impossibility, but hills made of earth and rock are quite suitable and widely used. Because this type of hill is rather large, it can be planted with trees and often has ridges, slopes, foothills, and stream-fed ravines formed of stones. Designers used many variables to create a rocky, uneven appearance like mountains in nature.

Solitary placed stones must be large and fantastically shaped. Taihu Lake stones meet this description. Because of the lake's proximity to Su-

znou, most of the famous stones in the city's gardens are from this lake. The famous Song Dynasty (960-1279) painter Mi Fu thought Taihu Lake stones very beautiful, praising them as "thin, transparent, wrinkled, and porous." The great Song Dynasty poet Su Shi added the term "ugly" to the description, here meaning fantastic and plain in appearance, and his contemporary the painter Xu Wenchang called them "alive," meaning that the stones seemed full of life, that even in their passiveness they expressed a feeling

of motion. Most Taihu Lake stones have a varied nature rich in abstract beauty. They are limestone, also known as green stones in China, quarried from Taihu Lake in the Suzhou suburb of Dongting West Mountain. Ages of flowing water and beating waves have sculpted many depressions in the surfaces of these great stones, giving them distinctive appearances. The smaller stones are often used to create hills. There is also a type of man-made hill consisting of yellow stone, a form of sandstone. This stone is abundant

Left: The stone stair cases for Guanyunlou Tower at the northeastern corner of Liuyuan Garden.
Below: The well garden rockery Zhouyunfeng (Hangzhou).

throughout southern China. It is formed of calcite joints, which give it a variegated surface that looks like it has been hewn by a sculptor or painted using the Song Dynasty landscape painting brush style which indicated the texture of rocks and mountains by light ink strokes. The stones' surfaces are fairly even and solid, making them suitable for piling up high when building lofty peaks or creating caves. This stone and Taihu Lake stone are the two most important elements used in southern Chinese garden hill construction.

The Functional Uses of Man-Made Hill Stones

Designers use man-made hill stones:

1. To form the backbone of the garden's terrain, thus becoming, along with water, a major scenic item; they were often topped with architectural structures, ancient trees, and other plants to draw attention to them.

2. To separate and organize space in gardens; also to screen, contrast, or frame scenery, or as a background for scenery, thus becoming a major element in garden design.

3. To create stone columns in courtyards or small scenes on hills when matched with pine and plum trees, bamboo, wintersweet, paulownia, peony, and banana and other plants; also on high terraces to give an unusual, majestic appearance, and with buildings, walkways, and pavilions to create scenery.

4. To create pond shorelines and to shore up slopes and earthen walls; also as flower stands to make manmade objects appear more natural.

Upper: Xiashan (Summer Hill) and a tower at back in Geyuan Garden, Yangzhou.
Right: The Xiashan and the Qingchi Pond in Geyuan Garden.
Below: The stone-made shore of a small pond in Yuyuan Garden of Shanghai.

The Lion-Shaped Stone of Suzhou's Lion Forest

The Lion Forest was originally a Buddhist temple garden built during the Yuan Dynasty of the 14th century. The garden's name came from a huge, lion-shaped stone found there. In the Buddhist sutras, Buddha refers to the laws as a lion roaring. The seat of the Buddha is known as the lion seat, indicating the great power of the Buddha. Therefore, stones resembling lions were selected to surround the garden's pond and to stand on the stone hill. Uniting the dynamic form of the lion with the religious idea of the Buddha declaring the laws created a special atmosphere unique among Chinese gardens.

The lion-shaped stones lack concrete details—they have no claws, teeth, or shaggy manes outside of those supplied by the imagination. As with the "untied boat" buildings, these stones are chosen for the images they evoke, not their fidelity; the emphasis is on spirit, not form. Natural stones that appear active in the midst of stasis—that look like a lion squatting, pouncing, or roaring—all

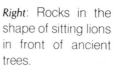

Right: Rocks in the shape of sitting lions in front of ancient trees.

Below: Artificial waterfall in Lion Forest, Suzhou.

Upper: The strangely shaped rocks are used to add a feeling of mountainous wilderness.

Left: A lion-shaped rock in a small yard.

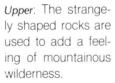

Upper: A group of dancing stone lions.
Left: A skilfully arranged rockery at Yuyuan Garden of Shanghai, known for its porous body.
Below: The lion seems roaring.

possess this spirit, an abstract character typical of Chinese classical art as in the "freehand brushwork" of classical painters. The expressive power of the stone lions varies depending on how and when they are viewed. Some should be seen from below, others from a distance. At sunset or in the moonlight, the fierce attitude of the lions is even more realistic. Originally, five ancient pines stood on the hill among the stones. These trees had strong trunks and twisting branches that, along with the stone lions, gave one the impression of being high in the mountains. The Yuan Dynasty founder and builder of the temple Master Tianru wrote a poem that expressed this feeling: "People believe that I live in the city, I believe that I live in the mountains."

Over the last six hundred years, Lion Forest Temple has fallen victim to many changes. Early this century the garden was changed into a private garden, the temple having ceased to exist long before. The existing architectural structures were built during the 1920s. Luckily, these Yuan Dynasty lion-shaped stones are still with us today.

Left: A winding bridge in the Huanxiu Villa of Suzhou leads to a deep valley.

Right: A gully in front of a square pavilion.

Lower right: Crape myrtle trees on a man-made hill in Huanxiu Villa.

The Total-View Man-Made Hill of Huanxiu Villa

This small garden, located in the rear of the residence, is set against a large hall. It contains the only remaining Taihu Lake stone man-made hill in southern China, and it is famous for its "total view" of peaks, cliffs, caves, and valleys. Though water makes up only a small part of the garden, it surrounds the mountain, and streams flow through the ravines. The garden was first built during the Ming Dynasty (1368-1644).

The famous garden designer Ge Yuliang added the man-made hill during the reign of Emperor Qianlong. It is now acclaimed as a masterpiece.

The main hill forms the center of the garden and is matched by a smaller hill in the northwest corner. It is composed of two sections: the northeast, an earthen slope inlaid with stone; and the southwest, a peak made totally of Taihu Lake stones. Outwardly, the hill appears to be only peaks, ridges, and precipices, but within it there are quiet caves and deep valleys. Stone-laid pathways wind up the hill. From within the valley, one gazes up at the imposing rock faces soaring into the sky and down at the stream gurgling below. At the top of the hill, a pathway circles the peak, and a stone bridge spans the ravine. A pavilion and walkway were originally located at the foot of the hill. Because the Huanxiu Villa is located in a residential district, there was little natural terrain that could be incorporated into the garden; therefore, ravines and valleys were built into the hill to achieve the large within the small.

Right: Bamboo and stone are used on both sides of the round gate of Geyuan Garden in Yangzhou to give a lovely spring scene.
Below: A small bridge winds in a man-made gully at Geyuan Garden.

The form of the hill is that of a natural mountain; consequently, it holds a high position in the history of hill and garden design.

Several ancient trees and many plants used to grow on the hill. The tree branches stretched high into the sky, adding grace and color to the hill. Unfortunately, the trees no longer exist; consequently, the hill's appearance has suffered greatly. To the east side of the hill, a series of ornamental windows are set into a white-washed garden wall which reflects sunlight upon the hill's stones. A long covered walkway, once located on the west side of the residence, had a tower at its end which offered a fine view of the garden. A pavilion at the edge of the pond and another near the hill are ideal spots from which to view the mountain.

The Hill Piling Art of Yangzhou

Hills of piled stone are the focal point of Yangzhou's gardens, but since there were no stones in the vicinity, all of those used in hill construction were brought in from far away. Ochre-colored yellow stones, blue-grey Taihu Lake stones, snow white Xuan stones, even stalagmites were used to create "four-scene" hills, each representing a season of the year. These "four-scene" hills are the principal characteristic of Yangzhou gardens. Because the stones had to be transported over great distances, few peaks were formed of individual massive stones; however, the lack of large stones is compensated for by the high level of artistry achieved in piled stone hills. Yangzhou's man-made hills are famous throughout China for their unique caves, valleys, and peaks. This section will introduce the Geyuan Garden's "four scene" hill, Xiaopangu Garden's caves and man-made hills, and the Heyuan Garden's "cliffs."

(a) The "Four-Scene" Hill of Geyuan Garden

This garden is in the rear of the residence and is reached via a narrow alley that runs along the side of the hall. Two large stone altars, one on

each side just through the entrance, are planted with bamboo and have surrounding columns of stalagmites. These altars represent the arrival of spring. The *ge* (个) in Geyuan resembles a bamboo leaf, therefore, its choice as the character in the name. Actually, bamboo takes second place to the man-made hill of stone.

After passing between the two altars and continuing through the garden's large circular entrance, one reaches the sweet-scented Osmanthus Hall. The pond in front of the hall serves as the garden's focal point. North of the pond, linked buildings and walkways extend around the east and west sides of the hill.

The summer scenery hill made of Taihu Lake stones stands in the northwest of the garden. The hill's face angles to the south and is covered with bamboo to match the green thickets of bamboo in the southwest section of the garden. A stream from the pond flows into a ravine in the hill and passes under an angled bridge before disappearing into a hillside cave. Caves riddle the hill and lead up to the peak

Upper: The stone chessboard in a cave through "Autumn" Hill in Geyuan Garden.
Right: The "Autumn" Hill piled up with yellow stone at Geyuan Garden.

where there is a pavilion from which one can sit and view the surroundings. Fantastically formed lake stones, running water and ponds, and the cool shade of caves and ravines give the sense of being deep in the mountains in summer.

The "autumn" hill is located in the northeast corner of the garden; it is made entirely of yellow stone. The hill faces west and on a clear day as the sun sets the hill turns red, highlighting the forms of its stones. This hill is different in nearly all aspects—layout, direction, stones,

form—to the "summer" hill. A large deep cave opens up in the middle of the hill. Light filters in on stones set up for chess play. A path leads up and into the cave, twisting and curving through the depth of the hill. There is a small courtyard on the hill, cliff walls tower into the sky, stone bridges cross open spaces, a pavilion stands on the hill's peak, pines grow up through gaps between stones. The hill-top pavilion against the northern garden wall offers a fine, but distant, view of the Narrow West Lake and its surrounding scenery.

Right: The "Winter" Hill at the Geyuan Garden.

Left: A small stone bridge leads to a cave in the "Summer" Hill.

In the southeast section of the garden, the Xuan stone hill faces north. The whiteness of shaded Xuan stone looks like snow, thus this hill's designation as the "winter" hill. The northeast wind that blows in Yangzhou rushes through a series of round openings in the wall behind the hill and makes whooshing sounds similar to the winter winds. Unfortunately, the winter hill has suffered a great deal of damage and has not yet been repaired; only a portion of the original hill remains.

The Geyuan Garden is centered on the "summer" and "autumn" hills; the "spring" hill with its many adornments and the "winter" hill with its impression of unmelted snow play a supporting role. The four hills stand independent of each other, yet provide interesting and complementary contrasts. Though there are many scenic objects, the garden is sufficiently large to avoid a sense of crowding. The designer, in setting the main scenic objects in the corners and along the sides of the garden, has maintained the effect of the empty core. Among the gardens of southern China, Geyuan Garden is the only one left of this unique design.

(b) The Caves and Man-Made Hills of Xiaopangu Garden

Xiaopangu Garden, though small, is famous for its cave. The garden is located at the east side of the official residence, its long narrow courtyard has a waterside pavilion in the center which divides the garden into north and south: the man-made Xiaopangu Hill occupies the northern section next to the garden's east wall;

Left: A scene of *ba-jiao* banana trees viewed from inside a cave in Xiaopangu Garden of Yangzhou.

Right: Man-made hill in Huanxiu Villa.

Left: The Ruiyun Peak at Liuyuan Garden of Suzhou.

Right: The porous Taihu Lake stone on a base.

the southern section originally had a large hill covered in flowers, trees, bamboo, and stone which offered a contrast to Xiaopangu Hill. One crosses a twisting bridge to enter the garden's cave. Its base is supported by thick, rough columns of stone. The cave has two entrances, one each at the north and south ends. The north entrance opens into the neighboring garden, and the south leads across a stone bridge to the other side of the pond. The cave divides the garden from what lies beyond; its doors and windows offer unique views of the surrounding scenery, in particular, of the stone lotuses and tigers in the pond.

The hill and buildings in the north were built next to the garden wall, their opposite sides face the pond. The architectural structures and hill cast their shadows far across the water of the pond which forms the "hollow" center of the garden. Pangu means "twisting valley"; the horseshoe-shaped hill made of Taihu Lake stones surrounds the garden's hollow center. Because the Taihu Lake stones which form the base of the hill extend into the pond, the buildings near the water seem to have their foundations in the pond itself. Fantastically-shaped stones lean against the buildings, bringing them into harmony with the man-made hill. Crafted stones of lotus and tigers dot the lake. Their expressive shapes and abstract forms bring the pond to life and match the weird shapes of the Taihu Lake stones of the hill. On the northeast side, the garden wall follows the contours of the hill, forming an undulating, twisting dragon of a wall.

Right: An undulating wall was built to serve as a foil to the man-made hill in the Heyuan Garden of Suzhou. The wall has decorative windows.

Of the gardens built during the middle years of the Qing Dynasty, several had small "twisting valleys," but the Geyuan Garden is the only remaining example. The Nine Lion Garden was an early "twisting valley" garden whose hill sported several abstract lions even finer than those described above. Unfortunately, this garden was destroyed in war at the end of the Qing Dynasty.

(c) The Art of the Heyuan Garden Cliffs

The western section of the Heyuan Garden focuses on water scenery, while the eastern section is noted for its cliff-faced hill. This cliff twists and undulates along the wall in the northeast of the garden. A "boat" hall in the center of the garden gives the impression of a craft traveling across land. The scenery is ingeniously designed, matching the water scenery in the eastern and western sections and offering contrast and harmony in appearance. However, rebuilding and repairs to the architectural structures in the garden were inadequate, and they no longer express their original intent. Only the front half of the cliffs still retain the atmosphere and form of long ago. This cliff and the cliff before the Five Peak Immortal Hall in the Liuyuan Garden are considered masterpieces of Chinese gardening.

The famous Ming Dynasty garden designer Ji Cheng remarked: "Use white garden walls as white paper

Left: The man-made hill at the Heyuan Garden was constructed along a wall. The whitewashed wall served as paper, while piled rocks were meant to be the painting. This marks a new creation in the making rockery.

Right: The Pipa Gate at the Zhuozhengyuan Garden of Suzhou shows that the building of a man-made hill along a wall can ensure wider space in the middle part and create a compact scene of an undulated hill and gullies.

and piled stones as colors and ink." Unfortunately, no cliff-hills of the Ming Dynasty exist today. The cliffs in the Heyuan Garden and the ones before the Five Peak Immortal Hall are both late-Qing Dynasty works, but both are artistic successes. In the Heyuan Garden, the designer placed an irregularly-shaped pond before the cliffs and provided a pathway that takes one up the cliffs for a magnificent view of the surrounding scenery. The body of the hill itself is unusually shaped—caves pass through its wrinkled mass, taking one deep into the maw and releasing one out onto the banks of the pond. A dragon-shaped, twisting wall rises where the hill turns to the east. The top of the wall, punctuated with windows, becomes an integral part of the garden's scenery. However, the portion of the hill and cliffs to the north has been greatly damaged by the passage of time and possesses little of its earlier glory. Originally, this section of cliff was rather small and decorated with flowers and trees in a visual reply to the stone hill and its pavilion and the "boat" hall.

By building the cliffs along the garden walls, the designer maintained a wide, open central space and at the same time created wonderful scenery of hills, valleys, and lakes.

The Large Man-Made Hill of Nanjing's Zhanyuan Garden

Zhanyuan Garden was originally the residential garden of Xu Da, the famous Ming Dynasty (1368-1644) general. It is located on the west side of the residence and was of great size, however, large portions of it

Upper: An earthen hill with luxuriant trees to the west of a pond at Zhanyuan Garden of Nanjing. The shore of the pond was built with stone.

Upper right: A curved stone plate bridge over a pond at the Zhanyuan Garden.

Right: A huge flat stone projecting into water.

were destroyed in the late Ming Dynasty. The remaining northern man-made hill still reflects the style of the early Ming Dynasty and is highly valued for its rock art.

The designer placed the focus of Zhanyuan Garden on this hill. A pond, streams, and architectural structures are designed to match the hill. The garden as it exists today is narrow from east to west and wide from north to south. The scenery reveals itself as one progresses through the garden. The main architectural structure, a large hall, divides

the garden into north and south sections. The hall is the center of touring activities and is also the best place from which to view the garden's scenery. A large grass lawn to the north of the hall once possessed a large platform planted with peonies. A pond separates the hall from the large hill, and a fan-shaped pond surrounded by bamboo, flowers, and trees is located before the hall's terrace to the south. The original pond was destroyed, and in recent times another hill was built, but the original design of the garden was never

restored. In the present garden, the hill in the north is set off against the pond in the south. They are balanced by the east-west contrast set up by the walkway along the garden's east side and the small man-made hill on the west side.

The garden's original northern hill was built of Taihu Lake stones; the pond at its foot was overhung by stone cliffs beneath which ran a stone path leading to a curved bridge, low to the water. Another bridge spanned a deep stone valley in the hill. A flat terrace crowned the

Right: Quietness is the first principle for building pavilions. This pavilion in the center of a pond at Xiyuan Garden of Suzhou serves as perfect example.

Right: Quietness is the first principle for building pavilions. This pavilion in the center of a pond at Xiyuan Garden of Suzhou serves as perfect example.

Left: The pavilions to the east of the Foxiangge in the Summer Palace of Beijing. Together with the hill and trees, they present a magnificent scene.

hill's peak and offered a magnificent view. These were all characteristic of the large Ming Dynasty hill. A wide, flat stone, low to the water at the base of the cliff, brought the viewer closer to the water and increased the contrast between the cliff and the flat stone beneath it. Water enveloped the front of the hill, further emphasizing its contours.

The man-made hill to the west of the pond consists mostly of earth; Taihu Lake stones are used only on the pond side to create a stone-shaped shore and hill slope, thus har-monizing this hill with the one in the north. The west hill is covered with trees and bushes in the center of which stands a small pavilion. A contrast is created between the soft, rounded shape of this wooded hill and the protruding, fantastic stones on its northern counterpart. Together, these hills produce a varied spectacle which is accentuated when seen as reflections in the pond they border.

10. The Art of "Emptiness" in Walls in Southern China Gardens

Many types of "empty" doors and windows frame breathtaking scenery that would be otherwise hidden from view. Some walls have windows, or "leak windows," making them semi-transparent and giving a misty, partial view of the scenery beyond and making the wall itself a decorative scenic structure.

The Art of Framing Scenery in Doors and Windows

Garden designers in southern China perforated walls with doors and windows to alleviate closed-in feelings, while at the same time allowing space and scenery to work together to draw the viewer into the scenery beyond. "Empty" windows not only allowed light to enter, but also the cool breezes to circulate. In Suzhou's gardens, each "empty" window offers a unique scene, a painting in itself. A small building or courtyard may be cut off from the outside, but is connected to it by the "empty" windows. Central China's gardens use the doorless, "empty" doorway to link courtyards and their scenery. By revealing glimpses of courtyard scenery, these doorways entice the viewer to enter. This tenet of garden design can be traced to Tang Dynasty poets who spoke of "opening the door to gain scenery" and said that "open windows lead into sights," here referring to the poets traditional concept of "making use of the scenery at hand." Designers created *dui jing* (comparative scenery) by erecting columns of stones or planting bamboo and plants to achieve "scenery beyond the scenery of the garden" which opened up the garden and emphasized spatial layering to achieve the artistic effect of seeing the large from within the small. *Kuang jing,* also known as "frame scenery," not only uses doors and windows to frame the views but also uses the frame itself as a decorative part of the scenery.

Open doors and windows look like picture frames and come in all shapes and sizes: square, oblong, round, oval, octagonal, hexagonal, vase-shaped, banana-leaf shaped, flower-shaped, fan-shaped, to name but a few. Most door and window frames are bordered with terrazzo tiles in delicate designs that express as much beauty as the scenery they frame.

Designers used door and window "frames" to highlight certain characteristics of gardens. For example, a frame concentrated on a flying eave,

Upper left: An ellipse gate (now destroyed) at the Huyuan Garden of Nanjing.

Upper right: The moon-shaped gate and lotus at the Canglangting Pavilion of Suzhou.

Left: The Haitang (Chinese flowering crabapple) Gate at the Lion Forest of Suzhou.

Right: The moon-shaped gate at the Ouyuan Garden of Suzhou.

Lower left: The moon-shaped gate at the entrance to the Jianchi Pond of Huqiu in Suzhou.

Lower right: The moon-shaped gate in a private residence.

Upper: A bottle-shaped gate at the Qianlong Garden.

Below: The moon-shaped gate at the Qianlong Garden of the Forbidden City in Beijing.

Upper: A bottle-shaped gate at Zhuozhengyuan Garden of Suzhou.

a column of stones, bamboo dancing in the wind, or the deep green of banana plant leaves could enhance small scenes which might otherwise be lost and lend them a lyrical quality. Also, designers framed distant mountains and rivers, giving the illusion that they were part of the garden and thus increasing its spatial limits. Often, bamboo, stones, plants, and flowers were placed in front of or around "empty" windows to create beautiful scenes in their own right. Because of the cold winds and short growing season, "empty" win-

dows and doors were seldom used in northern China's gardens, because their effects fell far short of those achieved in southern China. It was here and in central China that garden designers raised the use of the "empty" door and window to an art.

Decorative Window Art

The beautiful decorative "latticed" windows of southern China's gardens feature mostly flower patterns. They may be spaced close together or far apart, depending on the

designer's intent and the garden's layout. Though these windows do not give an unobstructed view of the garden, they do provide a double pleasure: examining the intricate craftsmanship of the windows can be as enjoyable as the enticing views they give of the garden beyond.

"Latticed" windows placed near the top of garden walls can relieve the monotony of an unbroken expanse. A tall wall crested by a series of "latticed" windows and fronted by hills, stones, and trees elevates an otherwise totally functional element

Left: An octagonal gate at Liuyuan Garden of Suzhou.

Right: A bottle-shaped gate and rectangular gate frame at Yuyuan Garden of Shanghai.

Upper: An octagonal gate at a temple in Hangzhou.

Left: A gourd-shaped gate at the Lion Forest of Suzhou.

Right: A broadleaf-shaped gate at Yuyuan Garden of Shanghai.

Right: The "latticed window" (no longer extant) at Liuyuan Garden of Suzhou.

Below: A view seen from an "empty window" at Liuyuan Garden of Suzhou.

Middle right: An "empty window" and a "latticed window" at Liuyuan Garden of Suzhou.

Right: "Latticed windows" at Liuyuan Garden of Suzhou.

Upper left: A "latticed window" of a geometric pattern formed with straight lines.
Upper middle: A "latticed window" of a geometric pattern formed with curved lines.
Upper right: A "latticed window" with straight and curved lines. The three windows are all found at Wangshiyuan Garden of Suzhou.

Upper: "Latticed windows" of different heights at Yuyuan Garden of Shanghai.
Right: "Latticed windows" of different shapes at Wangshiyuan Garden of Suzhou.

of the garden to a thing of beauty.

Most "latticed" windows are made of bricks and tiles, their depth is that of the surrounding wall, they have no protruding frames, and they are often the color of the wall—white. The flower-patterned frames in the windows are narrow and delicate across the front, but are the same thickness as the wall, thus creating a stereoscopic effect. When the sun shines through these windows it produces constantly changing patterns of light and shadow. At the same time, trees, bamboo, stones, and plants cast shadows that play across the white wall. Often these shadows and those of the "latticed" windows mix to present a fascinating tableau of shapes. The sun's movement and the vagaries of the winds passing through the garden keep all in perpetual motion.

Though the north side of an east-west wall is obviously the best for creating shadows through "latticed" windows, some of the same effects can be achieved on walls with a northeast-southwest or northwest-southeast orientation.

There are two types of "latticed" window patterns—curved line and straight line. The former is made with tiles, the latter with bricks and short pieces of wood. Both feature centralized patterns, the four corners coming together into a central figure. The curved pattern is marked by smooth, circular figures full of vitality and great variety. The straight line pattern is characterized by random shapes and irregular form. The curved line patterns possess a kind of movement in stillness, while the straight line patterns remain static.

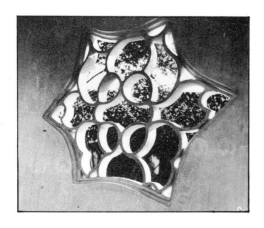

Left: A "latticed window" of Canglangting Pavilion in Suzhou.

Right: Another "latticed window" of the Canglangting Pavilion.

Below: "Latticed windows" at Xiyuan Garden of Suzhou (no longer extant).

Both can create rich effects through the interaction of light and shadow.

Most "latticed" window patterns are of auspicious or literary design. Patterns of pines, bamboo, and wintersweet are also common. Those that aren't made of brick or tile are formed of baked clay.

Many "latticed" windows are oblong in shape, but round, curved, multi-cornered, leaf-shaped, and pomegranate-shaped are also common. The great variety of "latticed" window patterns was limited only by the designer's creativity and the dictates of the garden the windows were designed to enhance.

Using different units to create various patterns was a common construction method. Designers achieved freedom and naturalness by combining a variety of shapes in straight line patterns, however, they could not adapt the same style to curved line patterns. Units made from colored glazed tiles were seldom seen in the gardens of northern China, but were widely used in the residences and courtyards of central China and the residential gardens of southern China.

Designers used appropriate formal contrasts—such as a square window between round ones—when placing

"latticed" windows, but they were careful to avoid excess. They believed window placement should include straight and curved line patterns both in close proximity and spaced wide apart—the goal being to achieve harmony in diversity. When a wall face had only one or two "latticed" windows, lively, free patterns were used such as leaf or fruit shapes. Where two windows in a small courtyard wall were of the same form, contrast was achieved through pattern spacing and the use of curved versus straight lines, just as change and vitality was created on hills and rocks by using the lines of branches and winding wisteria. Harmonizing variability and suiting scale to the local conditions were two principles that guided designers in creating classic "latticed" windows.

Part IV

11. A Survey and Analysis of Qing Dynasty Imperial Gardens in Beijing

Since the tenth century, through the Liao, Jin, Yuan, Ming, and Qing dynasties, Beijing has been the capital of China. The city's imperial gardens waxed and waned with each successive dynasty, but the gardens of the Qing Dynasty (1644-1911) were the greatest in number and scale. Most of the gardens that can be seen in Beijing today date from the Qing Dynasty.

Plenty of water is needed for building large-scale gardens. Arid northern China presented a great problem to garden designers. Fortunately, runoff from a range of mountains to the northwest of Beijing and the spring water from Yuquan (Jade Spring) Mountain in the western suburbs of the city supplied all the water the builders of Beijing's imperial gardens needed.

The clear water of Yuquan Mountain flows from many springs on the mountain. First it collects in Kunming Lake, then it follows the terrain and man-made channels, flowing from the north of the city into the city proper where it forms a series of natural lakes. The water enters the imperial gardens of the Forbidden City and the moat that surrounds it before flowing south.

The area around Beihai (North Sea or Lake) was originally a marshland with exquisite natural scenery. In the Liao and Jin dynasties (10th to 13th centuries), the emperors and their consorts began dredging ponds, building hills, and constructing gardens in this area beyond the palace walls. Qionghua Island is a product of this period; a palace was built on the island known as *Xian Dao* (Immortals Island).

Kublai Khan of the Yuan Dynasty (1271-1368) chose Beijing as his capital and called it "Dadu," the Great Capital. Beijing during the Yuan, Ming, and Qing dynasties was located on roughly the same site. During the Yuan Dynasty, the hydraulics expert Guo Shoujing planned the waterways system for the capital. Kublai Khan directed that the imperial palace be built around Qionghua Island and palace districts on the east and west banks of Taiye Pond.

After China was united again under the Ming Dynasty (1368-1644), all Yuan Dynasty palaces were torn down. However, a new set of imperial palace buildings were built on the east shore of Taiye Pond, and the area around the pond and Qionghua Island remained an imperial park.

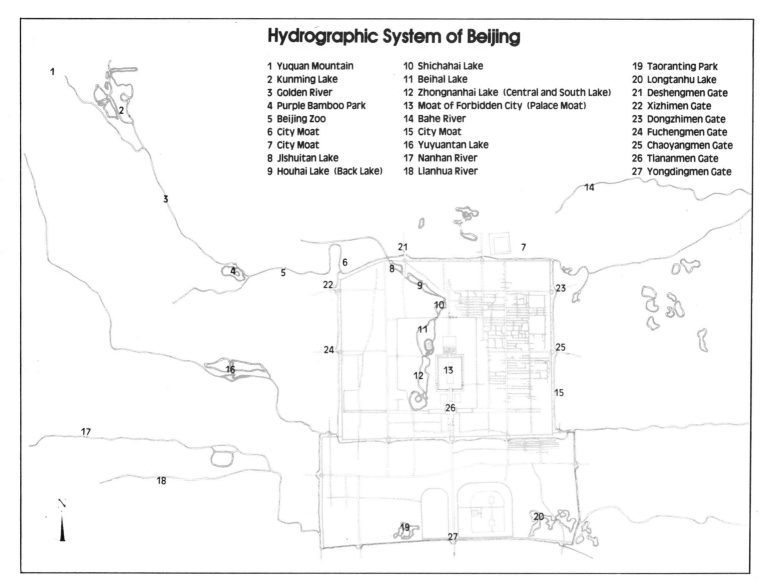

Hydrographic System of Beijing

1 Yuquan Mountain
2 Kunming Lake
3 Golden River
4 Purple Bamboo Park
5 Beijing Zoo
6 City Moat
7 City Moat
8 Jishuitan Lake
9 Houhai Lake (Back Lake)

10 Shichahai Lake
11 Beihai Lake
12 Zhongnanhai Lake (Central and South Lake)
13 Moat of Forbidden City (Palace Moat)
14 Bahe River
15 City Moat
16 Yuyuantan Lake
17 Nanhan River
18 Lianhua River

19 Taoranting Park
20 Longtanhu Lake
21 Deshengmen Gate
22 Xizhimen Gate
23 Dongzhimen Gate
24 Fuchengmen Gate
25 Chaoyangmen Gate
26 Tiananmen Gate
27 Yongdingmen Gate

The advent of the Qing Dynasty saw no major changes in the gardens and palaces of the capital. However, massive construction took place in the imperial gardens in the western suburbs. Emperors Kangxi (1662-1723), Yongzheng (1723-1736), and Qianlong (1736-1796) admired the natural scenery of hills and streams in the western district. There, they further exploited the waters flowing from Yuquan Mountain by constructing a massive garden with "three mountains and five gardens," namely, Wanshou Mountain, Yuquan Mountain, Fragrant Hills, Qingyiyuan Garden (on the site of today's Summer Palace, or Yiheyuan Garden), Jingmingyuan Garden, Jingyiyuan Garden, Yuanmingyuan Garden (also known as the Old Summer Palace), and Changchunyuan Garden. The Yuanmingyuan and Qingyiyuan gardens of the western suburbs, in particular, were extensions of the imperial palace in Beijing. The emperor spent most of his time in the government offices in these two gardens; only in the winter and on special occasions and festivals did he return to the Forbidden City in Beijing.

The Yuanmingyuan Garden was the largest of the gardens, but it was destroyed in the latter part of the Qing Dynasty by the joint forces of Britain and France. The Jingyiyuan and Qingyiyuan gardens were also destroyed, except for the large portion of the Qingyiyuan Garden which was rebuilt and renamed the Yiheyuan Garden, known today as the Summer Palace. ("Qingyi" means "clear lake water" and was chosen by the Emperor Qianlong; Yihe was chosen by the empress dowager Cixi

to express her wish for long life and wealth.) Regrettably, all the other gardens were destroyed and have not been repaired.

The Manchurian emperors of the early Qing Dynasty, unaccustomed to Beijing's summer heat, sought a cooler location for a summer capital. Later emperors settled upon the water-rich western suburbs and built several gardens there over a period of about one hundred years. They consumed a great deal of the nation's wealth and labor, building more and larger imperial gardens in the capital and the suburbs than any other preceding dynasty.

The emperors had gardens and palaces built in other locations besides the western suburbs including Pan-shan Mountain, Baiyangdian Lake and Chengde, to name but a few. These sites were chosen for their excellent scenery and terrain which allowed garden designers to create masterful combinations of natural and man-made beauty.

Qing Dynasty imperial garden designers not only carried on the traditions of northern garden design, they absorbed and copied styles and techniques from the famous residential gardens and architectural structures of southern China. The Kangxi and Qianlong emperors made six trips south between them, visiting the famous gardens and sites of central and southern China. Whenever something caught their fancy, they ordered their artists to make a drawing of it. The drawings became blueprints for the imperial garden designers. Also, many famous garden designers from southern China were summoned to the court in Beijing to

Upper left: A square pavilion at the Qianlong Garden of the Forbidden City in Beijing.
Upper middle: The imperial garden in the Forbidden City.
Upper right: A pavilion over a man-made hill in the forbidden city.
Left: A round pavilion at the Coal Hill, Beijing.
Right: A round pavilion at the Qianlong Garden in the Forbidden City.
Picture on previous page:
The Five Dragon Pavilions in Beihai Park viewed from Qionghua Island.

join in garden construction. Under these influences, Beijing's imperial gardens achieved a splendor never seen before or since.

Qing Dynasty designers stressed scenic planning and organization. Architectural structures were grouped together and placed in all corners of the garden. The concept of "scenery" was the major element in garden design, each imperial garden consisting of several different scenic areas.

Down through the ages, all imperial gardens possessed an "island of immortals on the seas" scene; Bei-

jing's imperial gardens also placed great importance on this element. Over two thousand years ago, the emperors of the Qin and Han dynasties sent emissaries to the "island of immortals" in search of an immortality drug. The fantastic scenery of the island of immortals, its buildings and pavilions, first appeared on the Taiye Pond of the Han emperor Wudi (140-86 B.C.). The South, Central, and North Seas (Beihai, Zhonghai, Nanhai) of Beijing were known by the collective name of Taiye Pond during the Ming Dynasty. Three "islands of

the immortals" were built in the lakes, Qionghua Island being the largest of them. Many Taihu Lake stones were placed into the dirt hill that forms the core of Qionghua Island, and in the middle of the island a stone-lined grotto was built, no doubt to enhance the fantasy of the "realm of immortals."

Prior to the Qing Dynasty, there were few religious structures in imperial gardens. The Manchu emperors and nobility of the Qing Dynasty believed in Lamaism, or Tibetan Buddhism, and in order to appease

the rulers of the Tibetans and Mongols they built several Lamaist temples and pagodas in imperial gardens.

The Three Seas of Taiye Pond: Beihai, Zhonghai, Nanhai

The Taiye Pond of the Yuan Dynasty consisted of only the Zhonghai and Beihai, or Central and North seas; Nanhai, or South Sea, was created in the latter years of the Ming Dynasty. This long and narrow series of lakes

was sandwiched between the Forbidden City and the Western Palace. (The western palace was destroyed during the Qing Dynasty.) These three lakes gave the imperial city's gardens an expansive, quiet, beautiful scenic area.

The three lakes were designed section by section, each with its own special scenic characteristics. The surface area of Beihai is rather large; Qionghua Island stands majestically in the middle of it. Zhonghai is extremely long and narrow with both shores crowded by a thick growth of

trees and plants that conceal elegant buildings. A small pavilion on the east bank adorns the peaceful, sedate scenery of this lake. Nanhai is small and circular and has a small island called Yingtai, meaning "Island of Immortals." A small hall on the island affords a distant view of the White Pagoda (stupa) in Beihai.

During the Ming Dynasty, Zhonghai and Nanhai were part of the Western Palace. Though the palace had a large number of buildings, most were hidden behind the trees lining the lakes which gave the

Left: The Tuancheng (Round City) Fortress and Zhonghai viewed from the White Pagoda of Beihai.

Right: A bird's-eye view of Beihai and Tuancheng (taken in the 1930s).

Left: The White Pagoda of Beihai.

Below: The bridge east of Qionghua Island in Beihai.

Picture on previous page:
The White Pagoda viewed from the northeastern corner of Beihai.

Below: A hexagonal pavilion at the Coal Hill.

Right: The Yunhuilou Tower, originally at Zhongnanhai, has now been moved to Taoranting Park.

Below: Square pavilions, originally in Zhong-nanhai, have now been moved to Tiantan (Temple of Heaven) Park.

Upper: The twin round pavilions, originally at Zhongnanhai, have been moved to Tiantan Park.

Left: The fan-shaped pavilion, originally at Zhongnanhai, is now located at Tiantan Park.

buildings a very peaceful, elegant appearance. Of the imperial architectural structures that now stand by these three lakes, most date from the period of Emperor Qianlong of the Qing Dynasty.

Of the three lakes, Beihai has the best scenery, its shoreline is irregular, its surface wide. Qionghua Island, near the southern end of the lake, is large and has a high elevation. It stands across the water from the Tuancheng Fortress. A long twisting stone bridge connects the shore and the island.

The Tuancheng Fortress is a large round terrace made of bricks. Several ancient pine and cypress trees grow high on the terrace, thereby balancing with the formidable bulk of Qionghua Island across the way. From the terrace one enjoys a magnificent view of Zhonghai and Nanhai to the south and the back of Qionghua Island to the north. This type of terrace pavilion was common about two thousand years ago during the Warring States Period (475-221 B.C.).

During the Yuan Dynasty (1271-1368), an emperor built Guanghan Hall, a palace symbolic of the moon, at the top of Qionghua Island. Here, nobility and ministers of that period enjoyed tea under the moon.

Early in the Qing Dynasty, at the request of the Dalai Lama, a Tibetan Lamaist pagoda, or stupa, was built on the ruins of Guanghan Hall. The hill was renamed "White Stupa Hill." The stupa stands out against the background of the sky and the foreground of the trees that surround it.

A Lamaist Temple in front of the stupa follows the hill's contours. Several pavilions, terraces, and buildings are located on the other side of the island. From White Stupa Hill, the highest point in the area, one can see all three lakes. Qionghua Island, Tuancheng Fortress, and Coal Hill, all located together and being the highest points in the Imperial Gardens, offer views of the garden's hills, lakes, and trees from various angles.

Several Lamaist temples on the north shore of Qionghua Island are hidden behind trees in order not to interrupt the wide visual expanse of the lake's surface. A bay in the lake extends in a northeasterly direction in order to enhance the flow of water into Beihai from Houhai (Rear Sea). This deep bay adds to the expansive appearance of the lake's surface, especially when viewed from the east side of the lake.

Near the north shore a group of five pavilions called the Five Dragon Pavilions stand in the lake across from Qionghua Island, grouped together in an arc and connected by a stone bridge. The center pavilion stands out above the others, the pavilions on either side descending in height. From here the five pavilions on Coal Hill to the east can be seen. When the Emperor Qianlong rebuilt Beihai, he paid special attention to the design of several small water scenes, creating secluded courtyard scenes in sharp contrast to the massive water scenery outside. He also insisted that each small water scene be different from the others. The crown prince undertook his studies in a small garden in the northeast called Jingqing Zhai (Clear Mirror

Hall), or "Qianlong's Little Garden." When the emperor gave this garden its name he wrote several poems, one of which referred to the meaning of "clear mirror." According to the emperor, the water in front of and behind the hall was bright as glass and capable not only of reflecting the structure, but also of mirroring the character and morals of a pure, selfless gentleman serving the people and heaven. The characters for "clear mirror," beyond their literal meaning of that which reflects, also have political and philosophical connota-

tions. Structures in Chinese gardens traditionally bear names which express multi-layered meaning.

The garden behind Clear Mirror Hall uses running water and its sound to create its hill-pond scenery. Because Houhai's water level is over one meter higher than Beihai, its water passes through a lock at the northern edge of Beihai and then channels through an earthen hill before entering at the east wall of the garden. Tumbling through the garden, the water makes a wonderful sound like fingers splashing over a

stringed instrument—a stark contrast to the still waters in front of the hall.

The first object seen upon entering the Clear Mirror Hall is a still pool of water to the north. A long, narrow strip of water runs behind the hall. An arched bridge and a column of rocks divide the garden's pond into three sections. The front pond is broadest across its middle where it is transversed by a walkway over the water. To the west of the walkway, a man-made hill and rock columns tower into the sky, a cave-passageway leads through the hill to

Upper: A small square pavilion and a hill climbing corridor to the north of Jingqing-zhai in Beihai Park.

Right: A marble bridge at Jingqingzhai.

111

a hexagonal pavilion at its peak.

During the Qianlong reign, Beihai was dredged and the earth was built up on the east shore to form a little winding hill. This hill is planted with trees, many of them peach trees, hence the hill is called Peach Blossom Hill. Up against the back of this hill, a series of small, quiet water-scenery gardens were built. Haopu Gully is located here. Its water is drawn from the northeast corner of Beihai to form a small interior pond. On the east shore of this pond, stones were piled to form an exquisite little

hill which conceals the east wall of the garden. A twisting stone bridge crosses the pond near its north end where a stone archway stands. A walkway from the veranda on the southern shore of the pond winds up the hill to a hall at its peak.

Following the larger earthen hill to the north from Haopu Gully leads to a building hidden among the hill's trees. This is Painted Boat Hall. It consists of four rooms with connecting walkways. There are very few architectural structures on the west shore of Beihai. It appears that the

east bank possesses only a hill and trees. In this way, attention is focused on Qionghua Island and the interior garden, where courtyards contrast with the island in a masterfully conceived and executed design.

Upper: The courtyard over water behind a man-made hill at Haopu Gully, Beihai Park.

12. A Survey and Analysis of the Summer Palace

Yiheyuan Garden, or Summer Palace, is located 10 kilometers northwest of Beijing. The garden measures 3.4 square kilometers of which the northern one-third is occupied by a hill 60 meters high. This area was a famous scenic spot before the Qing Dynasty. In 1703, a travel palace was built on the site, and, in 1750, construction began on a large-scale garden. At that time the garden was called Qingyiyuan Garden, or the Garden of Clear Lake Waters. Most of its architectural structures are located on and around the hill in the north known as Wanshou (Longevity) Hill. The name comes from the temple and pagoda Emperor Qianlong built on the hill in memory of his mother's sixtieth birthday. Taking the Emperor Wudi of the Han Dynasty as his model, Emperor Qianlong conducted naval exercises on Kunming Lake to the south of Longevity Hill.

After it was dredged and a causeway built along its eastern shore, Kunming Lake became one of Beijing's water reservoirs. In 1860, Qingyiyuan Garden was nearly destroyed by the English and French joint forces. In 1888, repairs were completed that preserved the original layout of the garden, and its name was changed to Yiheyuan Garden, or

Summer Palace. In 1903, most of the architectural structures were repaired, but those on the north face of Longevity Hill are only now being refurbished.

The designers of the Summer Palace took full advantage of natural hills and waters. For example, Longevity Hill is a natural hill with a base of natural stone. However, several of the stones on the hill are Taihu Lake stones, and some are stone slabs from nearby hills. These stones were arranged to form man-made hills and caves and to emphasize the ruggedness of the hill's ridges. Earth dredged from the lake was also used to build up the hill's eastern ridges.

Kunming Lake is also naturally formed, receiving its water from springs on Yuquan Mountain to the west. Dredging enlarged the lake to the southern slopes of Longevity Hill. Because the lake's waters also border the western slopes of the hill and extend to the north in a narrow pond called Rear Lake, it is almost as if Longevity Hill is an island.

The architectural structures in the Summer Palace are divided into four sections or zones. The first section, located east of Longevity Hall, consists of the East Palace Gate; the palace, including Renshou Hall; and, the

Upper: Huazhongyou, a group of pavilions to the west of Wanshou (Longevity) Hill in the Summer Palace.

Upper right: Foxiangge (Fragrant Buddha) Pavilion is the focal point of the Summer Palace.

Right: The Long Corridor at the Summer Palace.

official residential area. All these display the regal character of the imperial court. Walking from the hall, one rounds a hill of piled stone and suddenly Longevity Hill and Kunming Lake come into view. The Yuquan Mountain Pagoda in the distant northwest and the hills surrounding it form a magnificent backdrop for the garden.

The second section, in front of the hill, centers on the Foxiangge (Fragrant Buddha) Pavilion, before, behind, and to the west of which stand several groups of architectural structures. Foxiangge Pavilion is octagonal, four-storeys high, and built on a large, tall, stone terrace. A straight walkway at the center of the hill dominates the whole garden, directing the eye to a grand, colorful entrance at the bottom. The Foxiangge Pavilion, located along this walkway, has a courtyard that extends to the base of the hill and covered walkways on three sides. The pavilion stands on a great stone terrace, following the ancient method of building pavilions. The Foxiangge Pavilion is the garden's architectural center.

From high up on the pavilion, the lake—its islands, causeways, bridges, and boats—is captured in a view of man and nature in harmony.

The central walkway continues up beyond the pavilion, following the contours of the hill, until it reaches an exquisite Buddhist temple high on the crown of the hill. The Tibetan scripture Buddhist hall on the left and the copper pavilion on the right contrast markedly with the temple they flank.

In front of the hill, to the east and west, markedly different build-

Upper: The glazed-tile hall on top of the Wanshou Hill in the Summer Palace.
Upper right: A copper pavilion to the west of Foxiangge.
Right: A scene to the north of Wanshou Hill.

ings provide architectural contrast. On the east side, Jingfuge Pavilion looks south across the lake at the Longwang (Dragon King) Temple and the bridge of seventeen arches. On the western ridge of the hill, a series of pavilions and towers hug the contours of the terrain. Stone terraces climb the hill's slope and afford an excellent view of the lake and the distant Yuquan Mountain Pagoda. A touring boat on Kunming Lake provides a good perspective on the structures, trees, and stones that populate the Summer Palace.

A pavilion bridge from the stone "boat" at the western end of Longevity Hill takes one to the opposite shore. Here, a remarkable covered walkway 728 meters long lies at the foot of the hill. A balustrade of white stone parallels its length and links the hill's scenic points, as well as uniting the architectural structures that rim the front of the hill. The excellent views provided all along this walkway are perfect for enjoying the hill and lake, especially when rain or snow falls. The intricately carved stone balustrade rims the lakeshore,

allowing it to cast elegant shadows on the water.

Longevity Hill and Rear Lake make up the Summer Palace's third section. Here, mountain paths wind up the hillside. The Suzhou-styled river at the foot of the hill widens and narrows whimsically, its banks lined with trees and plants, the songs of birds in the air. In the past, Suzhou-style streets, shops, and buildings along the river allowed the emperors and their consorts, stepping off their touring boats, to feel as if transported to central-eastern China.

A group of Tibetan Lamaist temple halls and pagodas of colored tile, quite different in style from the architecture on the front side of the hill, are located on the hill's back slopes. After being destroyed by the armies of Britain and France, these structures were only recently restored to their former glory.

From the peak at the rear of the hill one can see Yan (Swallow) Mountain in the distance. In the spring, peach blossoms cover the hill, providing a spectacular sight unlike any available on the front side of the hill.

At the eastern end of the Rear Lake, a small garden in the style of Wuxi's Huishan Garden (today's Jichangyuan Garden) called Xiequyuan Garden (Garden of Linked Charms) was the emperor's favorite retreat in the hot summer. Towers, walkways, pavilions, bridges, and trees are reflected in the lake. The small water-scenery garden echoes the tiny Yang Ren Feng Courtyard in the eastern section of the garden. Both act as a foil to the glory and splendor of the larger garden, making them appear even more exquisite by comparison.

Upper: The Lamaist Halls (renovated in recent years) at the backside of Wanshou Hill.
Right: The pagoda built with glazed tiles and bricks at the back of Wanshou Hill.
Below: The 17-arch bridge over Kunming Lake.

The fourth section is Kunming Lake which occupies four-fifths of the garden. Its surface is unbroken except for a few small islands and one long causeway. Modeled after the style of those on West Lake in Hangzhou, this causeway has six little bridges of which the bright white of the Yudai (Jade Belt) Bridge is most visible. To the west of the causeway, the surface area of the water is divided into three sections, each with an island dotted with buildings and pavilions. These islands are known as the "Hills of the Gods Upon the Sea."

Buildings and other structures in the Summer Palace balance spatially. Designers placed closed-in courtyards in cols or at the foot of hills, concealing them in quiet, secluded spots; they placed structures that required distant perspectives in appropriate locations and paired them with exquisite scenery.

Designers crowned the roofs of major imperial halls and temples with colored tiles and resplendent green and gold inlaid designs and scenes; they designed secondary structures with roofs of gray tile and

117

lifelike Suzhou-style colored scenes. While individual structures in the Summer Palace follow official regulations regarding form and therefore lack variation and appear heavy, the designer's careful arrangement of them has resulted in a rich and varied architectural appearance.

The Jingmingyuan Garden of Yuquan Mountain

A leisure palace on Yuquan Mountain was first built during the reign of Emperor Zhangzong (1190-1209) of the Jin Dynasty (1115-1234). During the Qing Dynasty, Emperor Qianlong ordered the building of the Yufeng (Jade Peak) Pagoda on the mountain's peak in imitation of the Jinshan (Gold Hill) Temple pagoda in Zhenjiang, Jiangsu Province. The pagoda is nine storeys with a spiral stone staircase in its core leading to the top. The Summer Palace and Kunming Lake lay to the east of the pagoda, and in the distance Yuanmingyuan Garden (Old Summer Palace) is visible.

A small stone pagoda stands on the southern face of the mountain. It used to have a likeness of the Sakyamuni Buddha in stone relief. There are no large imperial halls, stupas, or Lamaist temples here. The Buddhist pagoda is of Song Dynasty style. The austerity of this site makes it quite different from other Qing Dynasty imperial gardens.

Yuquan Mountain is part of the Western Hills of Beijing. It is not a large mountain, but it possesses natural spring waters and delightful scenery. Springs well up out of cracks in the rocks and beds of sand all over

the mountain; the sound of gurgling water is always present. The name Yuquan (Jade Spring) was given to the mountain because the splash of spring water was likened to the sound of breaking jade. Spring waters flow off the mountain and collect in several small ponds. A pavilion on the mountain's slope allows one to look up to the pagoda on the peak, down to a clear pool of water below, and out to the beauties of Longevity Hill and Kunming Lake in the distance.

The Summer Palace and Yuan-mingyuan Garden near Yuquan Mountain are both large-scale imperial gardens, grand and imposing, crowded with scenic wonders. Yuquan Mountain, however, is a quiet, secluded spot, characterized by the scenery of the springs and pagodas. That the garden designers of the past, making full use of all the resources at their disposal, brought these different styles together into one integrated whole to create the grandeur of the imperial gardens of the western suburbs is truly a unique achievement in the history of gardens.

Left: The relief carvings on a small stone pagoda on Yuquan Mountain. The Heavenly King is in the center and on the sides are images of the Goddess of Mercy.

Middle: A whole view of the small stone pagoda. The Yuquan Pagoda is seen on the hill behind it.

Right: The small stone pagoda as seen from Yuquan Pagoda. (These three photos were taken in 1948.)

中国文化与园林艺术

胡东初　著

※

新世界出版社出版

北京外文印刷厂印刷

中国国际图书贸易总公司发行

（中国北京车公庄西路21号）

北京邮政信箱第 399 号　邮政编码100044

1991年（英）　第一版

ISBN 7－80005－128－5/ J.023

04500

85—E—370